BUILDING A POSITIVE SCHOOL CULTURE

BUILDING A POSITIVE SCHOOL CULTURE

CONNECTED, PROTECTED AND RESPECTED

BY

STEPHEN BROWN
The Brown Collective, Australia

AND

ANDREW FULLER

emerald
PUBLISHING

United Kingdom – North America – Japan – India
Malaysia – China

Emerald Publishing Limited
Emerald Publishing, Floor 5, Northspring, 21-23 Wellington Street,
Leeds LS1 4DL.

First edition 2026

British Library Cataloguing in Publication Data
A catalogue record for this book is available from the British Library

ISBN: 978-1-83742-094-0 (Print: Hardback)
ISBN: 978-1-83742-096-4 (Print: Paperback)
ISBN: 978-1-83742-093-3 (Online)
ISBN: 978-1-83742-095-7 (Epub)

INVESTOR IN PEOPLE

CONTENTS

FOREWORD

Allan Walker

Research Chair Professor of International Educational Leadership

Education University of Hong Kong

It's a pleasure to write this foreword for *Building a Positive School Culture: Connected, Protected and Respected,* written by Dr Stephen Brown and Andrew Fuller.

The authors rightly stress that in today's unpredictable and constantly changing world, schools are more than just places where students acquire facts and skills – they are lively communities where relationships, values and shared purpose influence every interaction. The role of the leader is therefore to shape and foster a school culture in which both students and staff, and indeed the leaders themselves, feel safe, succeed, are happy and are prepared for unknown futures. The strength of a school's culture can determine whether it merely functions or flourishes. When a school's culture is grounded in trust, connection and mutual respect, it becomes a powerful force that not only promotes academic success but also supports the emotional well-being of everyone involved. It is within this context that Brown and Fuller's *text* offers an essential guide for educators and leaders striving to create such cultures.

This book draws on Brown and Fuller's extensive experience working with schools across Australia and internationally. Their insights come at a time when educators face unprecedented challenges – mental health issues, the need for psychological safety and fierce competition for talented teachers and leaders. These realities underscore the importance of actively cultivating a school culture that is safe, inclusive and responsive. The authors emphasize that leadership is much more than managing policies or procedures; it's about shaping the relational core of the school community. It's about creating a space where trust and connection are not just aspirational ideals but everyday realities.

At the heart of their approach lies a simple yet profound framework – *Connection, Protection and Respect* – that guides the development and assessment of a healthy school culture. Drawing on extensive research and a wide array of feedback from students, teachers and leaders themselves, the authors demonstrate how these elements can be assessed and nurtured over time. But more than that, they remind us that culture is a living, breathing entity – ever-changing and requiring ongoing attention, courage and resilience from those in leadership roles.

A key theme throughout the book is the understanding that relationships form the foundation of resilience. Building trust, fostering safety and creating a sense of belonging are not peripheral activities – they are essential. The authors, applying Attachment Theory to school environments, emphasize how spaces that feel safe and accepting allow students and staff to thrive. When individuals feel genuinely connected and valued, they are more engaged, resilient and willing to contribute to the collective good. Conversely, when connection and safety are lacking, the fabric of a school begins to fray.

Leadership, therefore, involves more than just setting goals or making decisions – it is about the relational work of noticing, listening and responding. Leaders need to develop 'noticing' skills – being aware of subtle cues and signals that indicate the health of the school's culture. By paying careful attention to what is happening around them, leaders can reinforce positive behaviours, address issues early and foster an environment rooted in trust and respect. This intentional attentiveness helps ensure that connection and safety are woven into the daily life of the school.

Of course, fostering such a culture is not easy. It requires courage – challenging outdated norms, confronting 'sacred cows' and making space for difficult conversations. The authors cleverly use the metaphor of 'temple cats' – those entrenched policies, routines or behaviours that persist because they are unquestioned and unchallenged. Tackling these 'temple cats' demands resilience and moral clarity. It's about asking tough questions and being willing to shift mindsets, even when it feels uncomfortable. This kind of courageous leadership is essential if schools are to become genuinely equitable, inclusive and supportive environments where every child and adult can achieve their full potential.

Leadership also involves effective communication. The authors highlight that every decision and conversation shapes the culture. Successful leaders are skilled storytellers – crafting and sharing compelling narratives that embed values, inspire hope and foster a shared sense of purpose. Powerful storytelling can transform abstract ideals into relatable, emotionally resonant messages that motivate and unite communities. Alongside this, the quality of daily interactions – the conversations we have – plays a crucial role. Using Glasser's concept of 'conversational intelligence', the authors remind us that the tone, content and authenticity of our dialogues influence trust and safety within our schools. Leaders who can master the art of navigating difficult conversations and fostering open, honest dialogue can create the conditions for a culture of learning and mutual respect.

All these elements – relationships, courageous leadership, storytelling and mindful conversations – are interconnected. The authors offer practical, proven tools and reflective exercises to help leaders and teams assess their current culture, recognize areas for improvement and take deliberate action. They reinforce that culture isn't something that is ever 'finished' but a dynamic, ongoing process – shaped by one conversation, one act of kindness and one courageous challenge at a time.

The book ultimately invites us to see leadership through a relational lens – one grounded in moral purpose and everyday acts of connection, safety and respect. It urges educators to go beyond superficial initiatives and weave these principles into the very fabric of their work. When executed effectively, schools become spaces where everyone feels they belong, trust is cultivated, and both students and staff are empowered to succeed and realize their potential.

Why is this book so important? Because it doesn't just offer theories; it provides a practical guide for transforming school cultures into vibrant, supportive communities. It recognizes that culture is not a static achievement but a living organism that requires ongoing attention, moral clarity and resilience. Whether you're a principal, a teacher or a system leader, the insights and tools in the book can help you create cultures where everyone – children and adults alike – feels connected, protected and respected (CPR). When these elements are in place, schools become spaces of genuine learning, growth and hope.

Having said this, the book is much more than just a guide; it is an invitation to reimagine leadership as a relational act – one rooted in moral purpose and sustained through everyday acts of care and courage. The authors remind us that the true strength of a school lies in the quality of its relationships and the collective commitment to building a culture of trust, safety and respect day after day. The book's focus on daily practice sets it apart from other texts describing school culture and makes it 'real' for schools and their leaders. For anyone dedicated to making a meaningful difference in education, *Building a Positive School Culture: Connected, Protected and Respected* offers the inspiration, insights and practical strategies to turn that vision into reality.

As such, the book offers a valuable resource for educators, school leaders, system administrators and policymakers alike. I appreciate how the authors navigate complex ideas, offering clear, actionable guidance that can be adapted to diverse contexts. Whether you're leading a school, supporting teachers or shaping educational policy, the principles and practical strategies in this book will help you foster a culture that is not only high-performing but also humane, inclusive and resilient. It reminds us that at the core of every successful school are relationships – built through daily acts of connection, listening and moral courage.

In summary, the most insightful contribution of this book lies in three key ideas. First, it provides a simple but powerful framework – the CPR model – that helps leaders assess and nurture their school's culture systematically. Second, it emphasizes that building trust, safety and respect is fundamentally relational work – done through everyday conversations and interactions. And third, it offers tested, practical tools – storytelling, dialogue, diagnostic assessments – that enable leaders to translate these ideas into action.

We need more books like this that genuinely understand school life and explore key actions leaders can take to build equitable, future-ready schools by focusing on the core of school life – their cultures. Brown and Fuller have done a great job of pulling together their hard-won experience and academic knowledge in *Building a Positive School Culture: Connected, Protected and Respected*. I am happy to recommend it to anyone working in or supporting schools. I believe it has the potential to provoke thought, inspire action and contribute to a deeper understanding of the power of school cultures. I am confident that the book will not only deepen our understanding of school culture itself but also, if applied in context, can make a real difference in helping school leaders succeed in their ongoing quest to improve the lot, life and learning of their students.

ACKNOWLEDGEMENTS

A special thanks to my late parents, Shirley Elizabeth and James Vincent Brown, for providing me with the gift of education. Thanks to my wonderful life partner, Helen, for her unqualified support, encouragement and belief in me. Finally, thanks to the thousands of exceptional educators from around the world with whom I have had the privilege of collaborating in enabling the development of young people. This book is dedicated to each of you.

– Stephen Brown.

1

THE IMPORTANCE OF SCHOOL CULTURE: WHY DOES IT MATTER?

Positive, toxic, poor, nurturing – these are all prefixes that are used interchangeably to describe organizational culture or climate. They apply to organization's ranging from political parties, international sporting teams to government departments and schools. Such ill-disciplined and ill-informed commentary does add to the difficulty for school leaders in gaining clarity around a contested broad concept of organizational culture.

In the context of schooling, culture and climate are often used interchangeably without definition and distinction to describe arguably two of the most important aspects of enabling a positive and productive school. Although there is an acceptance of the importance of school culture to enabling school improvement, there is no agreed definition or construct of school culture and its distinctiveness or relatedness to school climate. Without such nuance, it is challenging to identify how school cultures can be augmented to have a positive impact on student learning outcomes (Australian Council of Educational Research (ACER), 2023).

School culture and school climate are distinctive, different but inextricably linked concepts. These concepts are what can be described as on the 'two sides of the same coin' (Hart, 2022). School culture and school climate are not the same thing. School leaders need to understand the differences and similarities between climate if they are to develop a precise approach to their approach to improving a school (Gruenert, 2008).

An organization's culture is typically described as 'the way things are done around here'. Culture is also about belonging, connection and being in relationship with others. It is 'a social narcotic of which all of us are addicted'. We feel good when we belong or relate to a group or tribe. It is an organization's anthropology – a system of interactions that governs how work gets done (Auron, 2025). Edgar Schein (1992) notes that culture is essentially a social indoctrination of unwritten rules that people learn as they navigate and connect with groups expressed in the workplaces as teams, peers and factions.

What are the components of any school culture? Many school leaders struggle when they try to describe the various elements of a positive school culture. It's tricky to define and parsing its components can be challenging (Shafer, 2018). School culture can be described as the set of shared beliefs, values and attitudes that shape interactions and behaviours within a school community.

Drawing on the foundational work of Schein (1992) and influenced by the perspectives of Vivian Robinson (2017), Dan Coyle (2018), Fiona Robertson (2020), Meg Wheatley and Tim Dalmau (1983) and Siobhan McHale (2020), these appear to be the fundamentals of organizational culture applicable to a schooling context:

- *Values and beliefs*: the core principles that guide the school's mission and vision.
- In the case of a Catholic School founded on a certain charism such teachings must be foundational to the culture of that school. How it then animates these will be through various mediating factors primarily stimulated, facilitated and stewarded by leadership.
- *Norms and expectations*: these are the unwritten rules in relation to how members of the school community are expected to behave. For example, attendance as school social, sporting and cultural functions and activities.
- *Symbols, rituals and artefacts*: displayed and deified things which give an insight or eyes to the soul of a school. These could include school honour boards, acknowledgment of the various community and cultural groups through ceremonies.

TYPOLOGIES OF SCHOOL CULTURES

To provide a degree of insight into the nature of school culture various researchers have articulated typologies of organizational and school cultures. Such classifications are useful in providing meta frameworks for leaders and observers of culture to provide insights into what are ways of 'doing things around here'.

The Competing Values Framework (Cameron & Quinn, 2011) notes that due to competing values at play in any organization, culture can be classified into four main types: Clan, Adhocracy, Market and Hierarchy. Cameron and Quinn used a two-dimensional dissection of competing values observable in organizations: flexibility versus stability and internal focus versus external focus.

1. Clan culture: There is an emphasis on teamwork, collaboration and a family-like atmosphere. It's characterized by strong employee loyalty, high levels of employee satisfaction and a focus on shared values and goals.
2. Adhocracy culture: This type of culture thrives in organizational settings that value innovation, creativity, curiosity and require participant adaptability.
3. Market culture: In such a culture, the focus is on achieving financial success and outperforming competitors. It prioritizes results and gains a competitive edge.
4. Hierarchy culture: Typifying this culture is a primacy of formal structures, clear lines of authority and a strong emphasis on rules, protocols, procedures and efficiency.

Every organization is uniquely shaped by its vision, mission, strategy, leadership and context. In their research published in Harvard Business Review article (January–February, 2018), The Leader's Guide to Corporate Culture, Groysberg et al. (2018) provide a broader classification of organizational cultures:

- Accountability culture: The predominant focus is on the establishment of a clarity of expectations, open communication and the development of shared ownership for achieving goals.

- Purpose culture: A culture that is driven by a strong sense of purpose and a shared understanding of the organization's long-term mission.
- Learning culture: This form of cultural dynamic places an emphasis on lifelong learning, the sharing of knowledge and a commitment to the development of its people.
- Coaching culture: Coaching is acknowledged as the major strategy to enable employee development and performance management.
- Constructive culture: Encourages positive interactions and a focus on employee wellbeing and self-actualization.
- Creative culture: Such a culture places and emphasis on innovation and the development of new ideas.

Context Matters

Same, same but different! Any school can be classified according to functionality, the ages of students it enrols, its governance arrangements, history and the geographical region in which it is located. For example, an independent Christian primary school located in a regional city, a specialist science school in a major city or a flexible school for re-engaging youth.

However, it can be argued that each school has a distinctiveness due to its culture – the way we do things around here. Culture is 'situationally different' (Beare et al., 1989). This is not surprising given the mix of complex variables and situational circumstances that interplay to contribute to a school's culture. Stoll (1998) notes that a school's culture is shaped by its context – its history, context and the people within it.

Taxonomies of school culture help provide insights and better understanding of the core activities such as teaching, learning and relationships within any school community intersect.

David Hargreaves (1995) notes that there are *several types of cultures* that can be observed in schools:

- *Collaborative cultures*: teachers work together, share the same educational values and are committed to improving their teaching and the school.

- *Comfortable collaborative cultures*: the school atmosphere is professional and although teachers are aware of the efforts of their colleagues, there is not a great deal of professional reflection.
- *Contrived collegial*: The tone of the school is determined by the leadership, which supports teachers' growth but on a superficial level which undermines motivation.
- *Balkanized*: The atmosphere is dominated by cliques of teachers that compete for resources and control. An 'us versus them' attitude between the staff and school's leadership team.
- *Fragmented*: Teachers all function independently and there is little collaborative effort to improve the school.

Stoll and Fink's (1996) profiled schools based on their *capacity to change*:

- Moving cultures: Dynamic, forward thinking and open to innovation.
- Cruising cultures: Stable but complacent, performing well but resistant to change.
- Strolling cultures: Lack direction; inconsistent performance and limited innovation.
- Struggling cultures: Facing significant challenges; low morale and poor outcomes.
- Sinking cultures: In crisis; urgent need for intervention and support.

Deal and Peterson's (2016) framework placed an emphasis on the symbolic and ritual aspects of a school's culture:

- Positive school culture: High expectations, celebration of success, strong sense of community.
- Negative school culture: Toxic relationships, low morale, resistance to change.
- Fragmented culture: Lack of shared values; isolated subgroups within the school.

In any organization such as a school there typically exists a range of microcultures or subcultures rather than a monoculture. Each school's culture and presenting climate will be a mix of many of the descriptors of the cultures outlined previously. There is not one point when a school's culture is fully aligned, exact and perfect. It is a continuous activity for leaders nurturing and nuancing school culture and climate. Robertson (2020, p. 71) notes:

> *There simply is no one 'perfect culture; there are only the desired cultural shifts that are needed for the unique combination of your culture (where you're starting from) and your current strategy (how you want to move forward with your team and organisation).*

Schools do not exist in isolation and are subject to the many social, political, economic and policy positions and trends that potentially will impact on any school's culture and climate. Brown and Duignan (2021) note that in an increasingly VUCA (Volatile, Uncertain, Complex and Ambiguity) or RUPT (Rapid, Unpredictable, Paradoxical and Tangled) world educators will be increasingly challenged by a tsunami of tensions, dilemmas and paradoxes that will only increase the complexity of leading any school. The narrowing of the school agenda to prioritize the focus on standardized testing regimes, the implementation by systems of a uniform approach to curriculum, teaching and learning; the constant tension of the provision of equity and or excellence are just a few of these. In shaping, nurturing and evolving any school culture, school leaders need to ensure alignment with and commitment to a stable core but respond adaptively to the issues disrupting and buffeting up against its edge.

What Then Is a School's Climate?

A school's climate refers to its current atmosphere as experienced by its stakeholders, or the operating environment of the school as reflected in the lived experience and interactions of students, staff, visitors, and others within the school. This could range from various forms of communication, workplace relations between staff, quality of leadership and simply, how it 'feels' to be associated with and to work in that school. A positive school climate is typically characterized by respectful relationships, a sense of belonging and a safe environment.

Conversely, symptoms of a negative, toxic or poor school climate are bullying, lack of student voice, low staff morale and a disengaged community. There appears to be consensus that school climate relates to individual perceptions and beliefs and the present or immediate (ACER, 2023). What can leaders or schools do to nurture school climate? Each school has a unique culture and prevailing climate, so any strategy adopted needs to be enabled after careful diagnosis. Such an appraisal should be on behalf of enabling a positive and productive learning environment for everyone.

The legendary band, Crowded House in their iconic hit song, Weather with You, evoke the importance of individual agency, mindset, responsibility, reciprocity and accountability for the collective, existing climate of any school and indeed organization. In essence, the song uses the concept of weather as a metaphor for a personal emotional state, highlighting that a person's internal feelings are a constant companion, and external changes won't necessarily alter their overall emotional state. In general, such an evocation reminds everyone that they are responsible for creating the around them – its energy, its emotional qualities, its positivity or negativity and its happiness and or indeed its misery.

Always take the weather with you. Every person who connects with any school is a 'Minister for Climate Change'. When everyone accepts this important portfolio, then a school environment is created in which everyone thrives. School climate is not passive – it is something by their practices, engagement, mindsets, energy, resilience and mindfulness that each person creates.

A school culture is influenced by the character of the individuals that make up its collective. Individual character is implicit and subjective, and stems from an individual's values, principles, beliefs and history. The etymology of the word 'culture' is from the Latin word 'Cultus' meaning 'to care'. Mark Twain notes that 'Everybody talks about the weather, but nobody does anything about it'.

School leaders need to apply continuous care to a school's culture and climate. Without attention and nurturing climatic conditions, shadow cultures will emerge and impact any school. School climate cannot be denied!

SHADOW CULTURES

One does not become enlightened by imagining figures of light, but by making the darkness conscious. (C. G. Jung)

Carl Jung arguably was the first writer to articulate the shadow concept as the one that is hidden, suppressed and denied aspects of humanity (Auron, 2025). Given that at the core of any organization such as a school there are people, it follows that a shadow culture(s) will exist. Such cultural shadows are cast when schools have stated values, but the actions of individuals or groups are at odds with these and community, societal expectations. Failing to act or covering up or not, addressing matters such as bullying, abuse of students and responding to issues that put at risk the safety of staff typifies this.

So where do school leaders start or place their focus in enabling productive thriving school culture and positive climates? We would suggest *'Below the Green Line'*.

The Six Circle Model devised by Margaret Wheatley and Tim Dalmau (1983) is a model designed to understand any organization such as a school from a system perspective and provides a framework of how leaders can effectively influence it. It divides the model into technical and relational aspects with a green line separating the two. '*Below the Green Line*' focuses on the beliefs, values and underlying assumptions that shape the organization's culture, evolving from individual and organizational histories and psychological factors.

The three circles *above the green line* are:

1. *Structure*: The ways in which a system such as a school or education system organizes itself to conduct its essential core activities or business.

2. *Operations*: The standard business processes that are used to build consistency and efficiency.
3. *Pattern*: Denotes the systematic approaches that any organization concentrates on delivering on its core purpose and core goals.

The *above the green line* circles are necessary but not sufficient to bring about sustained change and productive culture. The bottom or below the green line interconnected circles can be described as the social infrastructure of the organization. These are:

1. *Information*: The nature of work relationships is influenced by the quality of communication that is timely, inclusive and of value to enable people to do their work and feel connected to the overall direction of the enterprise.
2. *Relationship*: Any organization is a collection of people, and their behaviours, individual characteristics, beliefs and mindsets are instrumental to any organization's cultural health. People need to have open trusting and mutually respectful relationships.
3. *Identity*: Human beings are sense makers – we are informed, motivated and driven by our beliefs, values and sense of identity.

School leaders need to focus on both above and below the green line circles or aspects of their school. Our proposition is that the hardest and most difficult aspects of enabling and sustaining productive school cultures are 'below the green line' work – the things that influence how people interact and work together. The people work is the best work a leader will do and equally some of the hardest work that a leader will do.

Our connected, protected and respected (CPR) approach focuses on amplifying the below the green line aspects of a school relationship, personal identity and communication. The CPR approach will provide school leaders with a reliable, step-by-step process that has been researched and tested in schools to create positive cultures. This will be outlined in more detail in the following chapters.

Principals and school leaders play a crucial role in inspiring students, staff and members of the school community to continuously enhance the learning of everyone (Australian Institute for Teaching and School Leadership, 2011). Productivity Commission (2012) specifically highlights the importance of principals as cultural architects:

> *Principals have primary responsibility for setting their school's culture. They and their leadership teams provide the local foundation on which excellence in student outcomes are based.*

In a sense school culture and climate could be described as enigmatic, ethereal and elusive. Despite this lack of definition and specificity, school culture is seen as the critical aspect of enabling a productive, positive and performing school.

Our intention in writing this book is to support school leaders to explore and refine their capabilities to undertake this critical aspect of their work.

CASE STUDY 1: SCHOOL CULTURE – ST BERNARDS CATHOLIC PRIMARY SCHOOL

St Bernards Catholic Primary School was established 120 years ago in a regional city within Australian. 'St Bernie's' caters for students from Kindergarten ('K') to Six (6). Currently, the school has a student population of 456 students – the majority of whom are Catholic. The school is one of 65 schools that are a part of a Catholic education system. 'St Bernie's' staff typically were from the local area with long-term connections with the community.

In December 2023, the Principal, Bruce Strong, advised his supervisor that he would be taking leave from his role to deal with ongoing personal health issues and feedback from his supervisor that indicated that there were certain aspects of his principalship that needed improvement.

Mr Strong had commenced his first principalship 18 months earlier in July 2021. In December 2023, contact was made by the supervisor and head of human resources from the Dioecian office for support from an external consulting firm. In subsequent discussions there were several issues identified, and the perspectives offered indicated that the school's current climate and culture was toxic. This included the lack of cohesion in the school's executive team, inappropriate relationships between staff members that crossed personal and professional boundaries, a blurring of boundaries between staff and the information communicated to the broader community, no agreed and accepted professional expectations of staff members with respect to a code of conduct, a lack of a middle leadership structure, a minority of staff members who were outspoken and oppositional to change, a lack of quality in the teaching/learning practices within the school and a lack of formation for leadership support for key members of the executive. Mr Strong felt unsupported by his supervisor and a lack of tangible, decisive actions in relation to his perception of clear breaches of acceptable professional behavioural standards.

After a period of 12 months, the Principal, Mr Strong, returned to work, successfully undertaking the role of Principal. In the school's latest system-managed review of the school's climate, there has been a transformation in the indicators measured to an extremely positive set of ratings. How did such a turnaround occur? What interventions contribute to this relatively quick change?

A key first step was to work with the Principal, Mr Strong, through expert executive coaching and mentoring with the aim of affirming his capacity and giving him reassurance that he could return to the role. A related strategy was to use the expertise of the consulting firm to develop a theory of action to address the dynamics of the school's climate and culture. A crucial aspect of this was to respect his leadership and to leave the ownership of the work with him. Mr Strong with a degree of support from her employer successfully advocated for formal middle leadership roles and formal disciplinary action against certain staff members acting in ways unbecoming of staff at a Catholic school. Such steps then provided the Principal with the opportunity to launch his executive team and commence the processes of developing role clarity for team members. An important allied intervention was the co-construction with staff a code of conduct for all stakeholders of the school. These interconnected, deliberate and coherent steps enable a distributed model of leadership, people felt connected, they expressed an enhanced level of professional safety and that they had found their voice.

The exact context of this case study has been varied to respect the school, its community and wonderful staff.

CASE STUDY 2: SCHOOL CLIMATE – GLENVALE STATE SCHOOL, QUEENSLAND DEPARTMENT OF EDUCATION, QUEENSLAND, AUSTRALIA

School Profile

Glenvale State School is in the regional Queensland city of Toowoomba, Australia. The school is part of the Queensland State education system. The school was established in 1882 and has a proud tradition of excellence in education within a positive, caring environment. It provides comprehensive education to 766 students (2025) from the Preparatory year to year six. The academic, social and behavioural expectations at Glenvale State School are high. The stated vision for the school is 'we strive for Everyone, Every Day, Achieving Together'. The values of Glenvale are Responsibility, Respect and Safety.

Reflections: David Saxton, Principal

'We are ALL Ministers of Climate Change' (Brown, 2022). In my role as Principal of Glenvale Primary School in Toowoomba, Queensland, I reflected on the provocation by Dr Brown – an idea and insight that challenges each student, staff member, parent and visitor who walks through our doors to think about and reflect on the incredible influence we have on school climate and ultimately, school culture.

Each of us, whether we realize it or not, is a *Minister of Climate Change* in our school. We carry the power to influence the emotions and atmosphere around us every day, in every interaction, with our every word or action.

It is important to define what we mean by school climate and school culture – what is the difference and or connection between each of these ideas. *School climate* is what could be described as the atmosphere of our school – the mood, the tone, the energy that we experience in the various classrooms, hallways, offices and interactions we have on a daily or regular basis. *School culture* is much deeper; it's the shared values, beliefs and practices that guide how we behave as a community. While culture may take time to evolve, climate is something we shape moment to moment. We as Ministers for climate change, we're responsible for making the climate typified by support, continual growth and positivity.

Here's the truth: each of us brings our own 'climate' with us every day. Whether we're feeling positive, stressed, enthusiastic or frustrated, we carry that energy into our classrooms, our meetings and our interactions with students and colleagues. Our personal climate doesn't just stay with us – it spreads. It affects people around us. As *Ministers of Climate Change*, we must recognize and take accountability for this ripple effect. The climate we bring isn't just about us; it's about the impact we have on others.

So, how can we take ownership of our role as Ministers of Climate Change? Below are six strategies that we can all adopt:

1. *Check your 'climate' first*: Just like a weather forecast, you need to know your own 'climate' before you commence the day. Are you analogously bringing sunshine, warmth, clouds or storms? Deliberately pause and reflect. If you are carrying stress or frustration, take steps to re-set – whether it's through a quick breathing exercise, a moment of mindfulness or simply reminding oneself of our purpose – our 'why?' as educators.
2. *Be intentional about your energy*: Every interaction matters. A smile, a kind word or two, or even the tone of your voice can set and decide the mood for your students and colleagues. Similarly, negativity or impatience can cast a shadow that lingers longer than you might realize. Choose to bring the energy that uplifts others.
3. *Model positivity and resilience*: Our students are constantly learning from us – not just academically but socially and

emotionally. When we demonstrate and model optimism, perseverance and the ability to handle challenges constructively, we teach them life skills and help them moderate their own climatic responses in similar situations or circumstances.

4. *Own your own impact*: Accountability is key. If you recognize that your 'climate' is affecting others in a negative way, take responsibility. Apologize, if needed, reflect on what went wrong and make a conscious effort to do and be better.
5. *Support each other's 'climate'*: Remember, we're not in this alone. As a school community, we can support one another in managing our climate and climate change. Check in on our colleagues. Offer encouragement when someone's struggling. Celebrate small successes. By uplifting each other, we strengthen the overall climate of our school.
6. *Be the change you want to see*: As Ministers of Climate Change, it's not enough to notice what needs improvement – we must act. If you want a school climate that's more positive, more inclusive or more collaborative, led by example. Change starts with us!

The Bigger Picture

When we all embrace our roles as Ministers of Climate Change, we create a school environment where everyone thrives. Students feel safe, seen, heard and motivated. Staff feel supported, respected and valued. And together, we build a culture that reflects our shared commitment to excellence and compassion.

Remember, the climate isn't just something that happens to us – it's something we create. Let's be intentional about the change we're bringing and ensure it's one of positivity, growth and connection.

FOR REFLECTION AND DISCUSSION

1. Using the 3–2–1 Bridge Protocol (Project Zero, 2025), write down in relation to school culture, three key ideas/thoughts, two key questions and one metaphor or simile.

2. 'Travellers Eyes' (phrase attributed to colleague, Simon Banks) is a nice way to think about what you experience for the first time when you experience a school. This is analogously like the smells, colours, voices and temperature, for example, you first see or sense when you arrive in a new country or place for the first time. What did you experience with your Travellers Eyes when you first experienced your current school setting?
3. Like Travellers Eyes, empathy walks are a good way to get feedback from different perspectives on a school's culture and climate. For example, a parent for the first time gives feedback on how the school made her or him welcome and are their areas for improvement. What ways could you use empathy walks to support decision making, strategic thinking and or generally to refine your school's practices?
4. Using the various taxonomies of school culture presented in this chapter, how would you describe your school's culture and its current climate? Why do you hold this view. Discuss with members of the school's leadership team and or someone who supports your school.
5. How would you describe the subcultures that currently operate in your school or schools you have worked in? Why do you think they exist?

KEY IDEAS

- There is no agreed one definition of school culture.
- School culture and climate are different but interconnected.
- Various typologies of organizational and school culture – Cameron and Quinn (2011); Hargreaves (1995) to Deal and Peterson (2016).
- There is no uniform culture within a school – there exists subcultures and no one perfect culture.
- School leaders need to continue to nurture school culture – a core and important activity for every school leader but one

that is never complete. If leaders don't focus on school culture, one will exist and grow anyway.

- 'Below the Green Line' (after Wheatley & Dalmau, 1983) six circle model is useful for focusing the attention of school leaders. The three 'above the green line' are structure, operations and pattern. These are necessary but not sufficient to enable positive productive school cultures. The circles below the green line are the hardest areas but the enablers for culture – information, relationship and identity.
- The CPR model is designed to assist school leaders to work below the green line.

REFERENCES

Auron, M. (2025). *The shadow side of organisational culture*. www.culture.com

Australian Council of Educational Research (ACER). (2023). *National school improvement tool*. ACER.

Australian Institute for Teaching and School Leadership. (2011). *The Australian professional standard for principals*. Education Services Australia.

Beare, H., Caldwell, B. J., & Millikan, R. H. (1989). *Creating an excellent school: Some new management techniques*. Routledge.

Brown, S. (2022). *Leading the creation of a positive school culture*. Education Matters.

Brown, S., & Duignan, P. (Eds.). (2021). *Leading education systems*. Emerald Publishing Ltd.

Cameron, K. S., & Quinn, R. E. (2011). *Diagnosing and changing organisational culture: Based on the competing values framework* (3rd ed.). Jossey Bass.

Coyle, D. (2018). *The culture code: The secrets of highly successful groups*. Bantam Books, Random House.

Deal, T. E., & Peterson, K. D. (2016). *Shaping school culture* (3rd ed.). Jossey Bass, John Wiley & Sons.

Groysberg, B., Lee, J., Price, J., & Cheng, Y.-J. (2018). The leader's guide to corporate culture: How to manage the eight critical elements of organisational life. *Harvard Business Review*, *96*, 44–52.

Gruenert, S. (2008). *School culture, they are not the same thing*. Principal March/April. www.naesp.org

Hargreaves, D. (1995). School culture, school effectiveness and school improvement. *School Effectiveness and School Improvement*, 6(1), 23–46.

Hart, N. (2022). *Creating a strong culture and positive climate in schools – Building knowledge to bring about improvement*. Routledge.

McHale, S. (2020). *The insider's guide to cultural change – Creating a workplace that delivers, grows, and adapts*. Harper Collins Leadership.

Productivity Commission. (2012). *Schools workforce*. Productivity Commission.

Project Zero. (2025). *Explore more thinking routines*. pz.harvard.edu/thinking-routines

Robertson, F. (2020). *Rules of belonging – Change your organisational culture, delight your people and turbo-charge your results*. Major Street Publishing.

Robinson, V. (2017). *Capabilities required for leading improvement: Challenges for researchers and developers* [Research Conference]. http://research.acer.edu.au/cgi/viewcontent.cgi?article=1306&context=research_conference

Schein, E. (1992). *Organisational culture and leadership* (2nd ed.). Jossey-Bass.

Shafer, L. (2018, July 23). *What makes a good school culture?* Harvard Graduate School of Education.

Stoll, L. (1998). *School culture*. Reprinted from School Improvement Network's Bulletin. Autumn.

Stoll, L., & Fink, D. (1996). *Changing our schools: Linking school effectiveness and school improvement*. Buckingham Open Press.

Wheatley, M., & Dalmau, T. (1983). *Below the green line or the 6 circle model*. Unpublished manuscript.

2

HOW DO YOU KNOW THAT A SCHOOL IS THRIVING? THE CPR APPROACH TO SCHOOL CULTURE

The world our children will inherit tomorrow is born in the schools we build today. (Rabbi Jonathon Sacks)

Successful schools impart information, base themselves on relationships and build character and identity. Research conducted over the past five years compiling and factor analysing measures of thriving from 193,000 students and 800 schools identified the three main features of a thriving, positive school culture:

1. Connect
2. Protect and
3. Respect (CPR).

When people feel CPR as members of a school or of a community, they thrive.

Connectedness is the basis of belonging and secure attachment. This enables good learning, the creation of quality relationships and is the building blocks of mental wellbeing. This is why relationships are at the heart of great schools.

Protection is a sense that you can keep yourself safe and that others will also keep you safe. Feeling protected and safe enables people to be innovative, creative learners who 'have a go'.

Respect goes beyond manners and courtesy to the nourishing of strengths, aspirations and dreams. It is a message that every person in our community has a contribution to make, is asked to make that contribution and when it is made, it is valued and expected.

These three components intersect and mutually support one another to create a positive school culture (see Fig. 1).

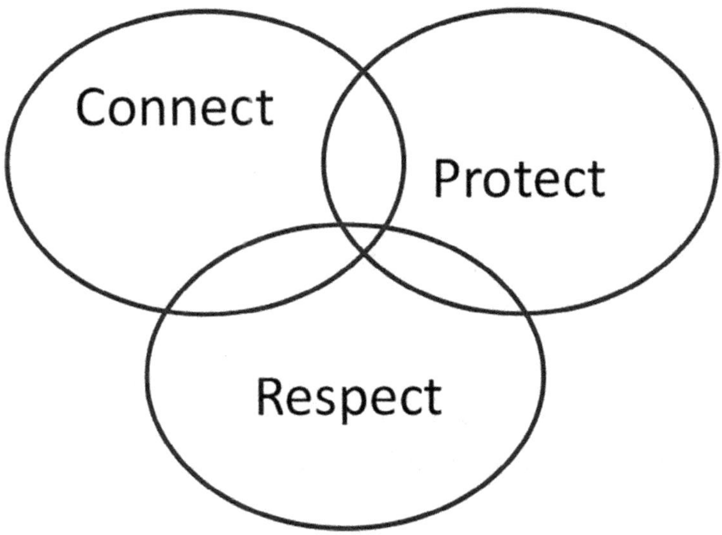

Fig. 1 The CPR Culture.

WHAT WE LOSE WHEN CPR IS MISSING

One of the ways of considering the power of each of these features is to conduct a reverse – analysis – to reflect upon what is lost or goes missing when each of these three components is not present.

Connect

When connectedness is missing in a culture, we found low levels of belonging. Belonging is one of the most powerful antidotes to loneliness, suicide and depression. It is a major underpinning of resilience and wellbeing and enhances learning.

Wellbeing does not come from running another one of the many (largely ineffectual) wellbeing programmes on offer; it comes from the heart of the school and community. Connectedness is embedded in the school culture and forms the basis for the way relationships are created and contributed to, by everyone. Linking to one another and being on one another's care becomes the cultural norm.

Lack of connectedness results in low levels of trust. Distrust in schools erodes collaboration and creativity. No one wants to stand out for fear they will be mistreated, ridiculed or rejected by their peers. This can lead to conformity and a stifling of identity formation.

The damage wrought by low levels of trust on learning outcomes is easy to imagine but harder to directly measure. Nevertheless, we can conclude that people don't learn positive things from people they aren't able to trust.

When we have low levels of connectedness, we feel wary, vigilant and concerned that we will be judged harshly by others. Playfulness, innovation and experimentation are diminished. The personal threat of making a mistake is high. People play 'safe'. Therefore, people either conceal the mistakes they (inevitably) make or don't attempt new things due to anxiety over failure.

Low connectedness is also related to low integrity. The absence of shared relationships lessens people's loyalty to following through on their undertakings to others. There is less integrity. Reputational damage is less of a consideration as there hasn't been much of a relationship built to begin with. No one really matters much to anyone else. This can result in people going 'missing in action', not following through on their commitments and also feeling their own contribution is either not important or relevant.

In cultures with low connectedness, we find higher levels of alienation. Many people feel overlooked or isolated. Many don't care about anyone else. There is a culture of meritocracy and hierarchy. Some people are seen as possessing attributes that are valued and celebrated. Others lack these desirable features and are disregarded. There is a sense of success for some, rather than a sense of success for all.

This in turn leads to a more individualistic culture. There is less teaming. Not only are achievements seen as reflective of individual accomplishments, but problems are viewed as reflecting individual ineptitudes. There is more blaming. This reduces collective and community problem solving.

Recognition of successes when they are achieved tends to be restricted to a few. This is the world of zero-sum games, of a few very clear 'winners' and a large number of 'losers'. The hierarchical nature of recognition lowers the self-efficacy of people in the community and results in increased comparisons between people and lowered motivation. Either you possess these valued attributes or not.

Protect

When a sense of being protected is missing from a school culture, no one feels safe. When people don't feel safe they tend to coagulate into cliques or tribes and identify some people as allies and others as enemies. This is the basis of 'us and them' thinking which underpins violent extremism, sexism, class-based entitlement, racism, prejudice and homophobia. The fear inherent in 'othering' some people not only destroys cultural cohesion, it dehumanizes us all. It limits our capacity to learn from people who are different to ourselves. If left unchecked, this can develop into scapegoating where a few culprits are identified and are viewed as responsible for all of the problems within the community. This consolidates a culture of shame and blame, lets everyone else off the hook from being responsible for creating a better culture.

'Us and them' thinking occurs when we regard people as members of groups rather than as individual people with feelings, ideals and values. 'Us and them' thinking in turn reinforces the need for wariness and vigilance.

Tribal thinking has been a successful survival strategy for humans. However, when it occurs in a school community it often causes friction, lowered care for the wellbeing of others and a sense of 'I need to look after myself first and so I don't have the (money/time/energy/resources/capacity – insert any excuse you like) to care for others'.

At times this is 'justified' by a form of predictive resentment – 'Even if I did have what it took to care for others, they wouldn't appreciate or benefit from it anyway'.

When tribalism is converted into hierarchies of worthiness and meritocracy, the damage amplifies. The entitlement of those with valued attributes can become a justification for the oppression of those without those qualities.

People who feel unsafe are on-edge and are prone to anxiety. They are also more anxious and distractible. It is hard to settle or concentrate on what you are being taught if you also need to remain alert for potential attacks or denigration by others.

Of course, for anyone in the community with a history of trauma, the negative effects are exponentially amplified.

If a loss of safety becomes a feature of a culture, people learn quickly to 'dim their lights', lower their aspirations and hopefulness and instead, endure and survive. Fear prevails and restricts what people can become. While we want our people to thrive, they will be focused on just surviving.

Respect

We often associate respect with the important practices of courtesy and consideration for others, but its implications reach far further.

Disrespect is demeaning. If we are demeaned, we are robbed of meaning. To live and learn in a culture that belittles your attempts is one that engenders conservatism and conformity. It robs people of their dreams. The dreadful result of low respect is in the threat of denigration. It doesn't even need to occur for its toxic power to have an effect. The anticipation of what other people might think and the judgements they might make is enough to clamp toxic limitations on many people's lives.

To be subjected to ridicule or sarcasm is a dreadful experience at any age but especially as a child, partly because the nuances of sarcasm are beyond the child's interpretative skills. Of course, for a teenager, being mocked and mistreated is excruciating. Lucky teenagers convert denigration into anger, unlucky ones convert it into self-hatred.

When respect is missing in a culture, people lower their motivation and aspirations and become dejected. Helplessness reduces resourcefulness. Helping and contribution to others is reduced because being seen as too compliant risks social ostracization. A sense of despair pervades and predisposes people to sullen depression and despair.

In a school, this can create a misty-eyed view of nostalgia where we should return to the basics and the 'good old days'. As the writer P. J. O'Rourke (1999) beautifully replied to people extolling the 'good old days', 'I've got two words for you – childbirth and dentistry'.

Instead, let's focus on creating the 'great new days'.

Being disrespected is an event that lingers long in people's memories; it echoes through their lives. Members of your community may not remember everything, but they will never forget the moments they were either shamed or belittled.

STARTING THE JOURNEY

Every leader starts this process with trepidation. Some of the forces against CPR appear formidable. The quest is creating a school with dignity and humanity. This is not idealism; it is pragmatism. If we want to live in a better world, we need to create one.

As Neil Postman once said, 'Children are the living messages we send to a time we will not see'.

A CHECKLIST FOR CPR IN SCHOOLS

Connect

Do people feel like they belong at my school?
Are people linked across different areas of the school?
Do people feel positive relationships are at the centre of the school?
How well does the school greet and include new members of the community?
Does the school take steps to include people who are marginalized?

Protect

Do people feel safe here?
Do people feel that others have their back?
Are people able to focus on their main roles (rather than watching out for issues directed at them from others).
Is wellbeing everyone's business and we are all in the care of one another?
Does the school have mechanisms for identifying people who may not be feeling safe?
Does the school have mechanisms for supporting people who may not be feeling safe?

Respect

Do people generally act in courteous and professional ways?
Does the school have a sense of meaning and coherence of purpose?
Are people's skills and strengths valued and called upon?
Are people treated fairly here?
Are the different contributions made by people valued or are their attributes possessed by an elite few who are preferentially treated?
Are mistakes seen as learning opportunities (rather than a matter of shame or blame)?
Is there a sense that the culture of the school is evolving to reflect the diversity of people in the community?

THE FEATURES OF A POSITIVE CPR CULTURE

Connect

Connection is the basis of belonging. It equates to integrity and trust. This requires an emphasis on forgiveness rather than coercion. Mistakes are made in all schools. It is how those mistakes are managed that determines the relational basis of the school culture.

For this reason, a CPR school culture promotes creativity, experimentation and a 'have a go' mindset. The emphasis is on constructive and innovative learning rather than rankings or critical appraisal.

Hierarchies are seen as unimportant. Instead, students are seen as having different types of brains and accordingly, the school differentiates learning to increase their chances of all students experiencing success in learning. It is not a case of fitting in or one size for all.

A CPR school culture builds an enabling learning culture and embraces development and change.

Protect

Protection enables people to feel safe in school. Physical and emotional safeties are essential prerequisites for learning. Relationships are seen as the very heart of a great school and quality relationships are the basis of maximizing learning.

As a result, it is not a punitive school. Shame and blame are not seen as appropriate strategies.

A culture of care and kindness is actively built and sustained through practising that we are all in the care of one another. Wellbeing is seen as everyone's business.

Respect

Respect goes beyond courtesy and manners to supporting one another's aspirations and not only strengthens relationships but also builds hope.

All members of the community are seen as being able to contribute to the wellbeing and learning of others. People are actively encouraged to make their contribution.

It is recognized that people will make different contributions depending on their capacity. Their contributions are actively invited and respected.

When relationships endure times of difficulty, the school actively practises relationship repair.

CPR is essentially about building and maintaining the positive relationships that allow people to reach their potential.

SECURING QUALITY RELATIONSHIPS

The success of a positive school culture directly relates to the way people treat one another. This means that great schools recognize that catalyst for creating great outcomes is to develop and contribute to quality relationships.

Research conducted by John Hendry et al. (2018a, 2018b, 2018c, 2018d, 2018e, 2018f) over the past 10 years, determined the five elements of quality relationships:

1. Trust
2. Forgiveness
3. Integrity
4. Hope
5. Kindness (or compassion).

Trust

Trust is fundamental to human survival. Our ancestors may have survived the odd scrap though competition, but it was the people who were able to cooperate and trust who lived well in tribes and that is why we are here today. Our ancestors trusted people.

We seek out trust. We seek it in our leaders, we seek it in one another and we seek to find it in ourselves. Trust is the cradle of security and the foundation of generous care for one another.

Trust promotes authenticity. It is the bedrock belief that this person can be relied on, depended on and trusted. Trust frees us to play, grow, be creative and be ourselves.

In all relationships there are pivotal moments when trust is tested. These can destroy or strengthen a relationship depending on how we manage these challenges.

Forgiveness

Once trust has been established in a relationship it is important to anticipate there will be times when it will be tested.

There will be times when all of us make mistakes, and our trustworthiness will be questioned. It is at these times that relationships will deepen through forgiveness. For this reason, forgiveness is the second element in quality relationships.

John Hendry points out that forgiveness means that you 'give-for' the relationship to exist and function. Forgiveness rebuilds trust.

Forgiveness allows us to heal and grow. It is not the part of us that has been hurt or injured that can provide the forgiveness. We need to call upon a larger sense of ourselves or who we are, in order to forgive. Being forgiving allows us to look beyond ourselves to the greater good for ourselves and others.

We all have been called upon to forgive. Who among us has never been hurt, let down or disappointed by other people. If we were truly unable to forgive we would be very lonely indeed.

Similarly, we have all been forgiven. We have all upset people, hurt another's feelings, said something unwarranted or hurtful or let down a friend. Anyone who has parents has been at some stage been forgiven by them. Anyone with friends has at some time been forgiven by them.

By acknowledging that we all have flaws helps us to see the flaws in others and forgive them.

Forgiveness is showing mercy to others and ourselves. Forgiveness is not conditional – it is transformational.

Integrity

The establishment of trust builds relationships, the way mistakes are forgiven cements it and when people act with integrity they build new pathways.

Wisdom is knowing what path to take integrity is taking it.

Integrity essentially is being who we say we are and doing what we say we will do. It is about being authentic.

People seek out integrity. They want ideas, people and actions on which they can meaningfully rely. They want to relate to people they can believe in. Integrity is the quality that answers the question, 'can I rely on you to do the right thing?'

People want to act with integrity and often feel ashamed when their actions don't match their words or ideals. The times when we lose integrity are often the times that haunt us most in life. Pausing to think before taking an action helps us to maintain our integrity.

Reputations are often ruined when people lose integrity by not acting honestly.

In relationships, integrity means that each person gives by behaving with the best interests of themselves and other people in mind. People know that they have a responsibility to act with care. The contribution they make, matters.

This means that people's actions are based on values rather than on situations or circumstances. Integrity is being true to your word, doing what you say you will do and acting in accordance with positive values.

When mistakes are made, these are acknowledged and accepted, and the people involved move to repair the relationship through forgiveness. It is understood that the intention of each person is to do the right thing.

When integrity is lost, trust is broken. It is replaced by suspicion, wariness and anxiety. These are the signs of fear. There are times in all our lives when fear is an ally. It can save our lives. However, when it dominates in a relationship fear saps trust and confidence. Hurt and resentment can tear away the best of relationships.

Guarded, distant or distrustful relationships bring us no joy or nourishment. These are relationships that either need to be changed or left.

Upstanders and Bystanders

Having integrity is not walking past when things are wrong. We don't allow people to be mistreated or bullied. It involves standing up for what we believe in and acting in accordance with those beliefs, even when it is difficult to do so. We do not stand by.

Acting with integrity is doing what we can within our power to stop people being hurt without doing harm yourself. If we do not have sufficient power, we notify those who do have the power to stop people being hurt. When we have integrity we show leadership and true friendship.

Hope

Hope is a sense of faith in the future and our ability to create better things.

The eminent psychologist, Rick Snyder (2003) found there are three main aspects to hope:

1. Being able to make goals for yourself.
2. Being able to devise strategies for reaching those goals.
3. Being able to remain motivated to reach those goals.

If learned helplessness is a predictor of the likelihood of depression, then 'learned hopefulness' is a powerful antidote. It gives hope.

The anticipation that good things will happen in the future and that we have the power to make some of those good things happen is hope. It makes a great difference to young people when the adults around them take on a position of hopefulness. At times, we all feel powerless and perhaps despairing. If you fall victim to hopelessness you hand over your power to the uncertain whims of the future.

Hope is the driving force that is left to us in bad times. It is the balm of the soul.

Hopeful cultures enable and hopeless cultures dislocate, disempower and disable.

Kindness

Kindness connects us to others. It is the wellspring for empathy, respect and caring. Kindness is a deep form of appreciation.

Kindness is natural and defines what it is to be human. We all possess mirror neurons that give us an empathic understanding of the feelings and actions of other people. This is something we are born with. It is innate.

Kind people are not those who lack flaws, the brave are not those who feel no fear and the generous are not those who never feel selfish. Extraordinary people are not extraordinary because they do not possess flaws. They are extraordinary because they choose to be self-aware and create a better world.

When present in relationships these five components provide an antidote to the alienated, unsafe and demeaning world many people live in.

HOW CPR CREATES A SCHOOL OF ATTACHMENT

Research from Bowlby and Holmes (2005) and Ainsworth et al. (2015) indicates that 45% of our students do not form secure attachments with adults. They neither trust the adults in their lives, including teachers nor do they trust themselves.

Their core belief is that people in the end will take advantage of you and/or harm you. This belief is confirmed when they err for their sense of shame indicates to them, in that context, that their belief about themselves holds true. When others err and it impacts them, their core belief about others is confirmed. They are reluctant to repair the relationships, they do not forgive or give themselves and they disengage the learning teaching connection.

About 20% of your school and community population will be avoidant in terms of attachment. These are students who have determined that they cannot reply on others and that being close to them is.

Another 20% will be anxiously attached. These people are not able to calm or regulate their own feelings and rely on others to help them soothe.

A further 5% have disorganized attachment, have usually has horrendous childhoods and then to make matters even worse end up having a series of tumultuous relationships.

School offers a second opportunity to develop a sense of security and attachment in life. Students who have not had the best relationships at home can attach to teachers, peers and to success and form a sense of security that has not been in their lives. This changes to life trajectories of those students because they learn in school how to create quality relationships something they may never have experienced in their earlier years.

Securely attaching students deepens relationships and contribution and frees people from the 'I'm happy, then I'm unhappy, then I'm happy again, then I'm unhappy' cycle that afflicts so many lives.

Similarly, some staff who have experienced attachment wounds in their own lives may find their workplace to be a balm to the troubles in their lives. Often these staff members are incredibly loyal and become devotees of the school.

Connected – while most of the research on attachment has focused on significant people in your life, we recognize that deep attachment can occur to family, community, mind and body, spirit/God, and nature.

Protected – people learn and live best when they feel safe and cared for, and where they are also able to care for others. It is in this culture that we learn best and can be adventurous and creative.

Respected – when we feel respectful as well as respected we can derive our own sense of meaning and develop a courageous and adventurous spirit.

HOW CPR AND CONTRIBUTION TURN A SCHOOL FROM A TEAM WITH A FEW CHAMPIONS INTO A CHAMPION TEAM

To create a school culture that can heal attachment wounds we need to develop teams that are worth attaching to and can sustain the five features of relationship when challenges arise.

Great teams and school cultures are built on trust and an understanding of one another's capacity to contribute. Culture is how we treat each other, how we talk to one another, whether we trust one another and how we handle differences and conflict. It is like an orchestra. The sum is greater than the parts.

Great school cultures are built on respect, on equal power, equal distribution and on the contribution each person makes. Some will make greater contributions because of circumstance or because of greater experience. One person may contribute more because they are more skilled, but every person is valued and respected and no one is belittled.

What great teams do is move everyone forward in contribution and those team members develop a sense of loyalty and trust in every member when mistakes are made. Great teams always give and take from every member and every team member is consistently being acknowledged for their contribution. They are encouraged to take risks.

We want our culture to encourage all community members to:

Show up ready to learn and perform.
Opt in and help out – make a contribution.
Be curious and interested.
Show others that you care.

To achieve this, we need to be in the care of one another. People in the team play for the team. We are interested in our collective capacity to create and sustain a great school. In a school if all staff are working for the common good of the students, overall achievement is better.

If we just become a group of skilled individuals, we just do our own thing for ourselves. We might get lucky, and we might create some great outcomes.

If we work together to become a champion term we‘re doing all we can to benefit the school and community. The sense of belonging not only protects all community members but also increases effectiveness. Greater capacity and co-operation create greater cohesion of effort. People who work for the team work above the capacity that they might show of they are just working for themselves.

In the next chapter, we'll review the main steps involved in creating a CPR school culture.

KEY IDEAS

- There are many competing models of school cultures.
- As outlined in Chapter 1, Cameron and Quinn (2011) differentiated between clan, adhocracy, market and hierarchical cultures.

- Hargreaves (1995) distinguished collaborative, comfortable collaborative, contrived collegial, balkanized and fragmented cultures.
- While Stoll and Fink (1996) profiled moving, cruising, strolling, struggling and sinking cultures.
- Each model offers a different lens through which to view school culture.
- The authors view quality relations at the heart of positive school cultures and therefore use a model of determining whether all people in a school culture are CPR.

REFERENCES

Ainsworth, M. D., Waters, E, Blehar, M., & Wall, S. N. (2015). *Patterns of attachment: A psychological study of the strange situation*. Psychology Press.

Bowlby, J., & Holmes, J. (2005). *A secure base – Clinical applications of attachment theory*. Routledge.

Cameron, K. S., & Quinn, R. E. (2011). *Diagnosing and changing organisational culture: Based on the competing values framework* (3rd ed.). Jossey Bass.

Hargreaves, D. (1995). School culture, school effectiveness and school improvement. *School Effectiveness and School Improvement*, 6(1), 23–46.

Hendry, J., Hawkes, N., & Fuller, A. (2018a). *Relationship-based education – The relationship quotient*. www.andrewfuller.com.au

Hendry, J., Hawkes, N., & Fuller, A. (2018b). *Relationship-based education – Trust*. www.andrewfuller.com.au

Hendry, J., Hawkes, N., & Fuller, A. (2018c). *Relationship-based education – Forgiveness*. www.andrewfuller.com.au

Hendry, J., Hawkes, N., & Fuller, A. (2018d). *Relationship-based education – Integrity*. www.andrewfuller.com.au

Hendry, J., Hawkes, N., & Fuller, A. (2018e). *Relationship-based education – Hope*. www.andrewfuller.com.au

Hendry, J., Hawkes, N., & Fuller, A. (2018f). *Relationship-based education – Kindness*. www.andrewfuller.com.au

O'Rourke, P. J. (1999). *Eat the rich*. Atlantic Monthly.

Snyder, C. R. R. (2003). *The psychology of hope*. Free Press.

Stoll, L., & Fink, D. (1996). *Changing our schools: Linking school effectiveness and school improvement*. Buckingham Open Press.

3

THE CPR APPROACH TO SCHOOL CULTURE: STUDENTS, STAFF, PARENTS AND COMMUNITY

The world often seems to treat people badly. It often disconnects people, dehumanizes, objectifies or reduces them into simplistic 'types' rather than allowing their humanity and complexity to be seen. The high levels of trauma in the world indicate how we fail to take care of one another. The friction and denigration that some people have in their encounters with others are not only discourteous and disrespectful, but also it leaves too many people in a shattered state of dismal fear.

The point we are hopefully conveying is that the world is not on your side in creating a connected, protected and respected (CPR) community.

In addition, schools have a form of immune system that makes them resistant to change.

As John Maynard Keynes once commented, 'Most people when confronted by a choice of changing their thoughts or proving there is no need to change, get busy on the proof'.

Creating a CPR culture will take intentionality and determination. It will take clear-headed strategy and most of all it will require the creation of quality relationships not often seen in the broader world. This is the reason we wrote this book.

This is not a process of trial and error. Not only is trial and error stupid, slow and expensive, it does no good practicing the wrong thing. To change a culture, we need to be systematic. If we want to do better, we need to get better.

The steps involved in creating this type of culture are clear. However, these steps are not linear. While we will outline these as simply as we can, each step is iterative, and you may need to cycle through some steps several times before sustainable change is achieved.

IDENTIFY THE COMMUNITY YOU ARE INTENDING TO INFLUENCE

While we'd like your school to become a role model for all other schools and positively enhance the power of education world-wide, we suggest beginning by tightly defining the boundaries of your sphere of influence.

Handpick a Small Team to Oversee the Process of CPR

While it is desirable to be inclusive, it is much more important to be effective. Select people who you can work with who are likely to bring a different perspective on issues, to yourself.

Select people whose discretion you can rely on.

If the community is very divided, it may be helpful to enlist an external facilitator as chair who can oversee the process.

Initially involve no more than seven people in the team. If you need greater representation, create additional teams.

Designate different roles within your team such as project manager, parent liaison, student voice, community relations, students voice, strategic analyst, opposition coach (black hat thinker – who should silently keep a list of issues, problems and limitations of ideas suggested).

Define in advance how the team will make decisions – consensus, majority rules?

Schedule regular meetings over at least six months.

If you are achieving one positive change every six weeks you are doing well.

Discuss how open or closed you want the team members to be regarding conversations and plans. While the initial analysis is being undertaken it is often best to be closed and then as your strategic change plan emerges to open up.

Outline some KPI's or milestones. How will you assess or measure these?

Promote adaptability. We may need to adapt and re-calibrate as we proceed.

Connect, protect and respect your team – create a support plan, if they receive criticism from the community.

ANALYSIS OF THE EXISTING CULTURE

The analysis progressively answers the following questions:

Connect	The current behaviours. What is happening?
Anticipate	The pattern or trend: What is happening over time?
Design	Underlying structures. What influences the patterns? Are there relationships between the patterns?
Transform	Mental models/values. What are the values, beliefs that support this? What beliefs keep the system in place?

Use these questions to guide an analysis of connect, protect and respect.

The purpose of an analysis is not to cure a sick culture but to amplify the strengths within the one we have.

Connect

How well do people connect with one another?

What is the level of care and friendship shown by people in my community?

How do we treat one another?

Are there people who are not treated well – who and why?

Has the pattern of connecting improved or worsened over time?

Are there trends that occur across a year or a term?

What are the structures within my school or community that either promote connections between people or highlight differences, hierarchies or create division?

What are the values and beliefs that sustain the current level of connection?

Protect

How well do we make sure people feel safe here?

How well do we make people feel safe to make mistakes?

Have the feelings of safety altered over time?

Respect

What are the indicators that the school celebrate the diversity of people and different ways of learning?

How well does the school differentiate learning to empower different learners to experience success.

SELECT A SMALL NUMBER OF NORMS TO START WITH

There will already be strengths and positive aspects of your culture and community to amplify.

You will discover even more as you progress. Keep a list of these. Eventually you will rank these and then place your highest impact in the change map outlined later in this chapter.

Things to diminish. It is likely there will be some glaring examples. While it is tempting to tackle them all, it is best to be strategic and intentional.

Outline the norms of behaviour you are seeking – what would be happening?

COMMUNITY WALK

You may do this is as a team or separately reporting back your findings.

Investigate and report back on the following:
Where do people naturally connect?
How are people greeted when they arrive?
Where do people feel safe?
What are the signs that people are respected here?
Where do people sit, relax and socialize?
How do people travel through the spaces?
How do they interact as they travel through the spaces?
What are the cared for spaces?
Where are the uncared for, spaces?
What spaces have potential but are currently under-utilized?
What spaces are available for community initiative?

If you were able to do three things to beautify or improve the environment of the community what would be your top priorities?

STRENGTHS MAPPING – WE'RE GOING ON A TREASURE HUNT

In almost every school and community there are hidden, under-utilized strengths. Don't limit yourself or your team with deficit thinking, start the treasure hunt for the overlooked abilities within your own community.

Let's begin by doing this on a community-wide basis. A model of this comes from Assets Building Community Development (P. Kenyon, *How to build community*. Personal discussion, 2025; Russell, 2022).

Select five influential people. Wherever possible this should be a different group of people to those within your CPR team.

Ask them to invite two other people who could contribute to strength mapping in your community.

Begin with the initial think tank of fifteen people.

Their task is to identify the strengths of the school or community.

Ask them to report back within a certain timeframe.

Don't be overly prescriptive about the form of the strength mapping.

One example is Table 1.

Table 1. The Head, Hand, Heart and Feet Diagram.

Head 	What knowledge do we have	What knowledge do we need
Hand 	What skills do we have	What skills will we need
Heart 	What passions do we have	What passions will be need
Feet 	What grounds us and keeps us authentic	What we need to ground us even more and keep us 'real'

Ask the group to report back their initial findings from discussing Table 1, and then expand their efforts.

Then, ask the 15 people to each invite 3 other people to the next think tank making a team of 60 to deepen and expand the inquiry.

Skills and expertise in your community – think about the people and organizations that could contribute to creating a CPR culture.

Facilities in the community – review what facilities are in your area who might be able to share skills and resources – parks, swimming pools, heath centres, businesses, local council, universities, other schools, hospitals, refugee centres, indigenous health centres and community services.

Natural strengths – this could include location, proximity, history, public transport, gardens, national parks

Expertise among the community – identify the specific expertise among school staff, family members. Perhaps there is a teacher is your school who is also a yoga instructors, perhaps there is a parent who could facilitate a drum circle or a business enterprise group. There may be a community member with skills on journalism and social media.

Potential partners – think about businesses and groups who could be good partners. Partnerships are a two-way process, with each contributing to the other.

Potential funding sources – think may take more time but consider what possible ways there could be to raise funds for renewal of community facilities or special events.

Finally ask people to name at least one strength that cannot be found easily. For example, the best place that has great coffee, the best place to talk to people you don't already know, the best place to read a book or people who are wise sources of advice.

School Staff Strength Mapping

While the external group are completing their review, you could consider asking your staff to identify their learning strengths. Ultimately this may include all of your students but for the time being let's involve the staff to gauge their reaction.

Ask them to go to www.mylearningstrengths.com and complete an analysis of their learning. While a complete report is available at a low cost, the initial email outlining their strongest learning strength is free.

Learning strengths aren't intended to limit the areas where team members can contribute to culture and performance, but they are a good place to start.

Many people will be capable in many areas. This is simply indicating an area they are already strong in.

Review with your team the spread of learning strengths, as shown in Table 2. Where are we strongest? Are there any learning strength areas where we are less strong? How can we capitalize upon the learning strengths of each other?

How could we use this with our students?

Table 2. The Mapping of Learning Strengths.

	Spatial Reasoning	Perceptual Motor	Concentration and Memory	Planning and Sequencing	Thinking and Logic	People Smarts	Language and Words	Number Smarts
Names of staff members with this strength								

IDENTIFY BARRIERS THAT SUSTAIN BELIEFS

The CPR team should then conduct a review of likely obstacles to change. This might be led by the opposition coach who has been considering likely objections, problems, limitations and disadvantages of ideas proposed so far, as shown in Table 3.

Protect this person. Their contribution in identifying likely issues is invaluable. It will be critical in anticipating and managing resistance and the immune system that resists change much easier for the group.

Brainstorm solutions to each major limitation.

There will always be in any group some people who think a cultural renewal is unnecessary and does not involve them. Think about ways to constructive call upon their contribution.

FINALIZE YOUR LIST OF INTENDED NEW CULTURAL NORMS AND ESTABLISH A TIMELINE

Now is the time to be decisive as a group. You can't tackle every issue at once, so you need to prioritize. Ask the CPR team to rank order the interventions.

Table 3. The Change Priority Mapping.

Big Impacts **Impactful with long-term impacts** Pareto Principle 80 of outcomes from 20% of undertakings What are the 20%	**Band Aides** **Things that will be impactful in the short term but may not sustain**
Quick Wins **Things that will be impactful in the short term**	**Energy Drains** **Things that are a waste of time**

CONSIDER THE MERITS OF OVERT OR COVERT PROCESSES

These aren't mutually exclusive but one you have decided upon your highest priority interventions you will need to think how to create what Gregory Bateson called 'the difference that makes a difference'. This is information that shifts perspectives and opens up new possibilities.

A parallel might be like driving a manual car. You can stay in one gear and just pump the accelerator harder, or you can change gears, increasing momentum.

Covert Methods

This includes nudge methods, noticing, rewards, modelling, rewarding approximation of preferred norms.

Neglecting unwanted norms or implicitly disapproving them.

Overt Methods

Develop a comprehensive communication plan. This will be outlined in Chapter 7.

Consider different groupings within your community – new students, senior students, other students, parents of current students, parents of potential students, staff, school board or council and community members.

Consider the most effective forms of communication for each group (these may overlap).

Develop multiple communication channels.

Whether covert or overt, the intent is to develop key concise messages to outline the benefits of the new norms. We will discuss this more in Chapter 4 on storytelling and Chapter 7 on communication.

AMPLIFICATION STRATEGIES

To amplify the CPR process in a school or community, you will need people who convey positive messages to others. We want to establish a new norm of 'this is how we go about business' here.

Not everyone in your community is equally influential. We need to think about who do we want to excite, who do we want to inspire, who do we want to influence or convince and who do we not waste our time on.

To do this we segment our population and then use inflexion points.

The precise percentages of each group will vary in different settings (see Fig. 2).

Early adopters are usually up to 2–3% of the community who are ready to support new ways of doing things.

Bright eyed and eager – usually about 13% of the community who are willing to embrace change but may not necessarily see themselves as drivers or contributors to that change.

I will if you will – usually about 34% of the community who are cautious about new changes.

While they are not necessarily resistant to changes, they will want to be convinced. Their over-riding sentiment is look at their peers and ask 'are you going to do it? Because if you're going to do it, I'll do it but if you're not going to do, I'm not going to do it'. Momentum of people will be important to getting them on board with changes.

Tricky people – these people can be resistant. Many have investments in the way things have traditionally been done and will either find suggested changes as fanciful or not relevant to them. You will need some way to directly benefit these people to either convince them or at the very least, not actively sabotage your changes

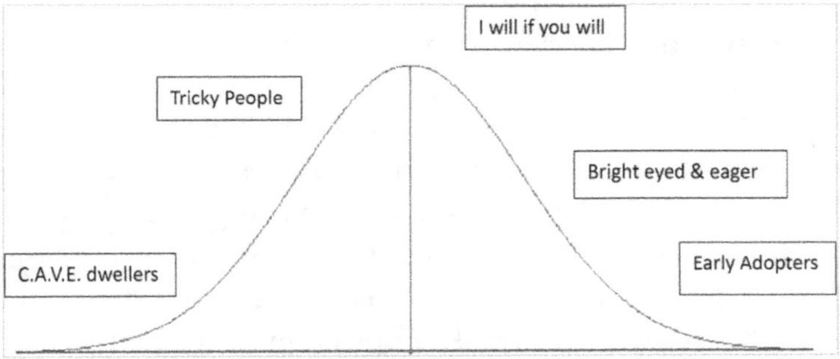

Fig. 2 The Normal Distribution Curve with Types of People.

CAVE dwellers – these are the Citizens. Against. Everything. No amount of convincing, cajoling, persuading or pleading will change them.

BUILDING MOMENTUM

This involves shifting from the leaders or the CPR change team to a broader range of connectors, protectors and respecters.

Inflexion points are change points that flip communities into positive contagion of ideas. These occur when 16% of a community embrace new changes and are willing to share thoughts and comments about the new ways of doing things.

To do this we identify the hyper-connected people in school communities. These are the people who seem to be known by everyone. Every school has at least a few parents who are well known among other parents, a few community members with links almost everywhere, a few students who are well known by their peers and a few staff members to thread and weave themselves across the different parts of the school and serve to connect people.

RINSE, WASH, REPEAT

The CPR team or just yourself can create a map of people in your community as shown in Table 4.

Making individual requests for help from hyper-connected people, especially in the early adopters and bright-eyed groups, to make general comments about the changes and to assist with implementation will increase the power of the inflexion points.

Make more specific requests of people in the 'I will if you will' group. Asking them to assist promote a specific idea or intervention. They may not see it as their role to get involved, unless you make a personalized request to them. Always follow up to see how it went and thank them and then, make a further request of them. Keep them involved, contributing and on-side.

Table 4. Community Involvement.

Activity	Already Involved	Not Yet Involved and Willing	Possibly Willing	Probably Resistant	CAVE Dwellers

DIGGING DEEPER

At this stage, you want to broaden your strength mapping process to the community.

Invite the strength mapping team to present their map and to conduct a workshop that delves deeper. As thorough as the team have been in their investigations, you will probably uncover buried treasures.

CONSOLIDATION AND SUSTAINABILITY

We often learn more from our successes than we do from our mistakes. Conducting a success analysis helps us to find what we are doing well and do more of it. This should not aim at noticing big successes but also mini successes.

How did you do it?
How did your figure that out?
Who helped or supported this achievement?

GET AHEAD OF THE RELAPSE

Of course, the heady days of early success will not be without their setbacks. Flies will find a way into the ointment. Clouds appear in even the sunniest of skies.

The frantic, chaotic maelstrom of school life will create a reversion to past methods. Students will misbehave, staff will feel threatened, some parents will complain.

This is the hold 'em or fold 'em moment. Implicitly, the community is asking you, 'are you really serious about this change or is this just another form of window dressing?'

The time for being firm in following through with your intentions is upon us. The metaphor of a sea captain steering a ship through stormy seas remaining at the wheel and setting the direction, springs to mind.

CELEBRATE THE WINS

Cultural change is an ongoing improvisional art. In a world where people are often inclined to think more about what they don't want, than what they do want. This chapter has encapsulated the steps of shifting to a CPR culture.

In the next chapter we will discuss how leaders can build a positive school culture.

FOR REFLECTION AND DISCUSSION

Cultural change requires sustained implementation over time.

Write a success statement for yourself.

What would my school culture look like if I was totally successful in achieving these changes?

Backtrack from that outcome and create a timeline with key indicators to assess whether you are progressing sufficiently or whether you need to incorporate different approaches.

You may opt for having a core team with several subsidiary teams work consecutively of different aspects of this change.

It is more important to achieve these changes thoroughly and successfully rather than quickly.

KEY IDEAS

- The CPR process outlined in this chapter appears in a step-by-step linear fashion.

- While it can be helpful to follow the process as outlined, it is not essential.
- Each part of the process is recursively linked and there may be times, you will need to repeat or deepen some steps to create sustainable change.

REFERENCE

Russell, C. (2022). *The connected community: Discovering the health, wealth, and power of neighborhoods*. Berrett-Koehler.

4

HOW CAN LEADERS BUILD A POSITIVE SCHOOL CULTURE?

School leadership is a significant variable in the determination of the nature of a school climate and impact on its culture. The individual leadership capacities and mindsets of school leaders will determine its performance. Equally, school culture 'makes or breaks leaders' efforts to bring about improvements' (Hart, 2022). It is a key factor in the impact of approaches to improving a school. Thacker and McInerney (1992) found a significant correlation between school culture and student achievement, thereby making the case that any school leader must consider a school's culture and climate as a critical factor in enabling any change initiative(s).

How can leaders build productive, positive school environments in which everyone feels connected, protected and respected and the school thrives? The most important question for leader must answer is 'What is the optimal environment for this group of perform to their best?' (Eastwood, 2022).

What do leaders do to create a sense of belonging and connection to their workplace in which they have voice, feel safe and valued?

Leaders should be obsessive about school culture – never complacent and satisfied that a school's culture is optimal.

The establishment, nuance and maturation of any school's culture is an ongoing process that will never be complete but paradoxically an aspiration that continually needs to be pursued. Deal and

Peterson (2016, p. 223) suggest that all school leaders need to consistently ponder three core questions: (a) what is the culture of the school now – its history, values, traditions, assumptions and ways? (b) what can we do to strengthen aspects of the culture that already fit people's images of an ideal school? and (c) what can be done to change or perhaps reshape when we see a need for a new 'bearing'?

The first place to start with for any leader is to be reflective, to be self-aware of their strengths and areas for further development.

RAISING LEADER SELF-AWARENESS

Leadership is a lifetime learning activity. Given the act of leadership is carried out by a diverse range of individuals, each being ultimately fallible, imperfect and profoundly human, then this must and should be the case.

Leaders must commit to learning as a fundamental to enable their growth and maturation in the art and practice of leadership:

> *Leadership and learning are indispensable to each other. (John F. Kennedy)*

We all have the capacity to inspire and empower others as leaders, but we must first be willing to devote ourselves to our personal growth (George et al., 2007).

> *Knowing others is intelligence; knowing yourself is true wisdom. Mastering others is strength; mastering yourself is true power. (Lao Tzu, 6th-century* BC, *Chinese Philosopher)*

In most organizations, most people are doing a second job – spending time and energy covering up their weaknesses, managing other people's impressions of them, hiding their inadequacies, uncertainties and limitations (after Kegan & Lahey, 2016).

Leaders must accept and wrestle with a presenting paradox or tension that no one will be the perfect leader, but everyone should aspire to be one. We are all imperfect leaders:

> *The truth is that we all imperfect [...] Imperfect leadership is about acknowledging our own and other's flaws, learning*

from them and even loving each other a bit. (Foreword, Hargreaves in Munby & Bretherton, 2022, p. vii)

All leaders should be their authentic self – bringing their best gifts, strengths, mindsets and unique personal story to their work. We learn in context, and we learn in relationships with others. Therefore, every new situation and every interchange with other people provide us with the opportunity to shape our leadership further. Moreover, every situation contributes to the building of a school's climate and impacts aspects of culture.

A key trait that all good leaders share is self-awareness underpinned by self-reflective practices. The best leaders are the best reflectors. The Centre for Creative Leadership (2025) notes that leader self-awareness is the number one trait for any leader in any organizational context.

Self-awareness is a foundational trait that forms the basis for other leadership skills and behaviours. Leaders who are more self-aware have a mature understanding of their strengths, short coming and areas for further growth. High-performing leaders are conscious of their personal biases, values, motivations and the impact of these on their decision-making; tend to have better emotional intelligence that enables them to be building positive, resonant, 'in tune', professional relationships (after Boyatzis). They are more adaptable adjusting their leadership approach in response to the context, feedback and the capabilities of the individuals, teams and stakeholders they are engaging with; build trust and credibility because they are seen as authentic and genuine; are usually effective communicators and constructively address conflict.

'If you can't read the room, you can't lead the room' (S. Brown, Linked In post quote, August 5, 2025). This quote evokes the importance of emotional intelligence of any leader to engage with others.

Dobrygowski (2016) suggests that 'self- reflection requires you to question your assumptions and habits and ask whether they are useful in dealing with the world around you. What are questions that school leaders should consider as a basis for self-reflection and to enable them to gain greater self-awareness? Here are initial questions and support strategies that school leaders can consider.

What Is Your 'Why' as a School Leader?

Always 'pivot back to your purpose'. A leader's 'True North' or 'North Star' is their orientating point derived from deeply held principles, beliefs and values. Nicholsen (2013) poses this as the 'compass question' – What is the gravitational force or reference point that pulls a leader in one direction, rather than another?

The Australian Professional Standard for Principals-Professional Profiles (2020) note that one of the professional areas in school leader practice is understanding self before leading others. School leaders need to surface and make conscious their values that inform their individual professional vision and narrative.

A leadership credo or narrative invites leaders to write and share their core values, beliefs about education and their purpose. A useful set of questions to ponder in enabling the development of such a personal vision are: (a) what do I care about? (b) what do I want? (c) what gives me professional life and joy? (d) what do I believe is the purpose(s) of schooling? (e) what do I believe about the students and staff I work with? (f) what do I believe about the parents, community in which I work? and (g) what do I believe about the system or sector of schooling I am employed in?

Such an artefact should also be written in a draft and continually reviewed. When we question what we are doing as educational leaders, we should always pivot back to our purpose – our personal narrative or credo.

A leader after reflecting on the core questions above can express concisely a credo or personal vision such as:

> *I do this ...*
>
> *... because I hope to.*

The articulation of a credo helps inform and make conscious for a leader their professional identity – the foundation of any leadership and leaders' development. Why? School leaders who develop a strong professional identity can improve their leadership effectiveness. Lowney (2003) amplifies this when he notes that 'a leader's greatest power is her or his personal vision, communicated by the example of her or his daily life'.

How leaders perceive themselves can impact on how they play out the role – the decisions that they make and their interactions with others. It can also impact both negatively and positively the motivation and behaviour of the people they lead.

Are You Still Curious and Courageous?

Do you still have the desire, the drive and interest in asking these important questions that you do not have the answers to? These are the questions that will be challenging, confronting, but necessary to explore to enable the growth and development of the school you lead. Bushe (2013) notes that individuals, teams and organizations such as schools and society evolve in a particular direction that they collectively, passionately and persistently ask questions about. Heifetz and Laurie (2001) note that one can lead with no more than a question in hand. School leaders need to stay and be curious. Being curious means being vulnerable, open to learning and asking or engaging with questions that they don't know the answer. A useful refrain for leaders to adopt and to stay curious is 'I don't know but together when can find out'.

One strategy that enables leaders to frame those tough, curious questions is the adaptive leadership framework that focuses on leading in situations where there are no clear solutions or where existing ones are not effective. Such circumstances sometimes require courage and a commitment to raising expectations. The refrain from Lieutenant General David Morrison (former Chief of the Australian Army) he uttered in 2013, is one that is useful to continually reflect upon – 'the standard you walk past is the standard you accept'.

School leaders need to continue to ask those challenging questions with the aspired intent of improving outcomes for all students and staff.

What Is Your Internal Dialogue?

Muhammad Ali, the iconic sportsman and social activist, noted that 'the fight is won far away from the witnesses'. A key reflective practice for you as a leader is to listen to your inner dialogue. What is your inner voice saying? Typically, such dialogue will focus on time, motivation and relationships. Such thoughts and feelings can be positive, negative and at the extreme, debilitating. In working with tens of thousands of leaders, managing and moderating inner dialogue is a significant issue.

Good leaders will develop practical strategies to manage, cultivate and at times, quell this voice. These include engaging with a coach, mentor, learning to embrace 'your weird' (after Crowe) and to remember the refrain 'you are enough' to enable positive self-talk. The longest conversation anyone will have in their life will be with themselves. Alain De Botton (2019, p. 63) notes that the origin of the inner judge is simple to trace: it is an internalization of the voices of the people who were once outside us.

Leadership cultural change requires resolve, a capacity to maintain self-belief and enabling work that contributes to the 'common good'.

Who Is On Your Leadership Team?

Leadership is not a solo sport. What kind of support team do you have to assist you in leading? A useful strategy for all school leaders to consider is establishing a personal Board of Directors (after Collins & Porras, 1994). Typically, a Board of Directors would have directorship for a peer, cheer leader, connector, coach/mentor and innovator. These categories can be moderated and augmented depending on the needs of each leader. A personal Board of Directors helps us to navigate those liminal spaces, sustain our energy for leadership, help navigate ethical dilemmas and support a leader's individual growth. Adam Grant (2023) in his text, *Hidden Potential* notes that all leaders and individuals need various forms of scaffolding such as mentors to enable growth and potential to be realized.

How Do You Capture Learning as a Leader?

'We do not learn from experience. We learn from reflection on experience.' The seminal framework of John Dewey (1910) is one that is a useful tool for leaders to 'catch their learning'. His taxonomy of questions is of:

- What? – What was the situation? What happened?
- So what? – So, what worked or did not work? So, what is the impact?
- And now what? – Now what will I do differently? Now what are my next steps?

This framing set of questions with other related strategies such as coaching, Board of Directors, feedback in various mediums are useful ways to enable leadership development.

Nicholsen (2013) notes that the self is a work in progress. It is a hall of mirrors. Leaders can claim it as their own and take command. This is some of the hardest work that a leader will ever do. The challenge for each of us as leaders is to turn reflection into practice.

Leadership is 'a verb, discovered in action and demonstrated in application' (Westfall, 2019). Our growth as leaders should be continuous but never complete. The curriculum of leadership is before a leader every day, you learn the work of leadership by doing the work.

Augustine Rodin's iconic bronze statue, Le Penseur, *The Thinker*, was recast 28 times since the original in 1902. The challenge, analogously, is not dissimilar to the one we face as leaders. We need to evolve, refine and look at the same subject ourselves from different perspectives.

Good leaders ask great questions. For our renewal and continuous development as a leader, we need to engage in self-reflection based on asking ourselves core questions – questions to lead by.

What are your questions that you need to focus on?

UNDERSTANDING SELF AND LEADING OTHERS

Leadership is about being in relationship and working with others.

What does leadership mean in leading any school and how does such a view influence a school's culture and climate?

The exercise of and the nature of leadership should go beyond formal positions and authority in a school if a culture is to be nurtured and continue to be refined. A school leader needs to adopt a distributed, invitational and inclusive approach to leadership. Schools are too complex for the leadership to be left to a small number of people in formal roles.

So, what do people want from leaders?

The demands of leadership are complex, but the foundation of a good leader is rooted in meeting the needs of those who follow them (Gallup, 2025). What do your staff, direct reports and stakeholders want from you as a school leader? Goffee and Jones (2000) in their seminal article posed the provocative question, why should you lead anyone?

Survey data (Gallup) indicates that only 15% of staff in workplaces are engaged with the single biggest factor driving such discontent being inadequate leadership (O'Keeffe, 2023). The Global Leadership Report: What Followers Want for the World Governments Summit 2025 in collaboration with Gallup examined this very question in groundbreaking research. The study (Gallup, 2025) identified four needs of followers – hope, trust, compassion and stability.

Let's explore each of these and their important these for school leaders in shaping, nurturing productive school cultures:

1. *Hope*: The need to feel positive about the future and for leaders to provide a clear direction. Hope? Followers wanted their leaders to provide inspiration, have a vision and display personal integrity. Such leaders created conditions that allowed for personal growth, learning and achievement. They felt supported, had agency and were connected to the aspirations of the organization. School leaders are between the past and the future. They need to have a sense of foreseeability, being able to articulate a collective vision for the future and create a school culture that cultivates imagination typified by the wonder of a child and the art of possibility, not limited by imposed boundaries. The Australian Council of Education Research (2023) School Improvement Tool identifies one of the first steps in enabling school improvement is the development and articulation of a shared approach or theory of action – an agreed, shared contextual approach to advance the school's performance.

In the face of the fast passed dynamic of leadership in schools, there will always be the challenge to act in the now but with an 'eye' to the future. Lowney (2003) suggests that leaders imagine an inspiring future and strive to shape it rather than passively watching the future happen around them. They extract gold from the opportunities at hand rather than waiting for the opportunity to be handed to them. School leaders need to develop and refine their strategic thinking professional capabilities – a prophetic ability to continually discern and reflect upon future possibilities.

2. *Trust*: The need for honesty, respect and integrity. The attributes identified were communication, approachability and trust. These were conveyed through collaborative practices, teamwork and compromise.

   According to Rath and Conchie (2008) co-authors of the text *Strengths-based Leadership: Great Leaders, Teams, and Why People Follow* note that creation and establishment of professional trust is at the core of creating relationships – the foundation of a quality professional school culture and climate.

   What is professional trust? While its importance and relationship are recognized, there is no one agreed definition or view about what it means.

   Maister et al. (2001) in their work, *The Trusted Advisor*, trust that there are four objective variables to measure trustworthiness – credibility (professionally competent), reliability (complete agree actions, tasks and role requirements), intimacy (being able to share authentically information and viewpoints that will never be compromised by inappropriate sharing) and underpinned self-orientation (the degree to which any leader or individual is acting in self or collective interest).

   In the context of schools, Browning's (2014) research identifies practices that leaders could develop to enrich a culture of trust in a school: admit mistakes; offer trust to staff members; adopting personal self-management strategies such as remaining calm and level headed, actively listening, providing affiliation; being present and visible; showing care for staff members; mentoring and coaching staff; making informed but consultative decisions and keeping confidences.

3. *Compassion*: The need to feel cared about and listened to. Such dispositions are noted as emotional intelligence, compassion and wellness. Service, altruism, mentorship and support were seen as expressions of leadership compassion. We need to be tough on issues but kind to the people we lead. However, we need as leaders to be much kinder to ourselves as well as the people we lead.

   Compassion is more than empathy. Compassion moves beyond an empathic desire to gain an understanding of engagement – acting in a way intentionally to make things better. Staff feel a greater sense of connection and belonging (Hull & Moore, 2025). Moreover, research shows that leaders who adopt a compassionate approach to people enable a greater sense of employee loyalty and trust (Seppälä & Cameron, 2015).
4. *Stability*: The need for psychological safety and secure foundations during times of uncertainty. Critical indicators for followers of this need were the provision of stability, structure, accountability and the acceptance of responsibility. Parks (2005) notes that throughout human history, within every social group, there is a hunger for authority that will provide orientation and reassurance, particularly in times of stress and fear. Quality governance practices are a fundamental aspect of productive school culture. Good governance is typified by such maxims as consensus orientated, accountable, transparent, effective, efficient, equitable, inclusive and follows the law (OECD, 2015).

It is an enabler in insuring and assuring others about any school's purpose and attention to such core accountabilities as child safety, professional standards of teaching practice, student performance and behaviour.

School leaders need to be obsessed with culture and the immediacy of school climate. They need to be 'first class noticers' (after Bennis, 2014) consciously paying attention to the dynamic in the school-observing, questioning and scanning the internal as well as the external school environment. As noted above, school leaders need leaders who have a clarity of personal values and aligned behaviours. A caveat to this worth noting is that leaders who impose their values too strongly risk creating 'facades of conformity' (after Hewlin et al., 2015). Moreover, according to Bennis (2014) emphasizes should model intellectual humility: (a) acknowledging limitations and recognizing that their knowledge is incomplete and that they are open to having their beliefs challenged; (b) be open to new information – display a willingness to consider, contest and engage with new, diverse ideas and evidence; (c) have the ability and desire to change – to refine, reflect on their perspectives, values and assumptions in response to new ideas and broader perspectives; (d) avoid being intellectually superior and arrogant; and (e) be a learner and stimulate a school culture that has learning as the cornerstone of a school's culture.

RESPONSIBLE STEWARDSHIP

School leaders are temporary custodians of the schools they lead – they hold a school temporarily in trust. Leaders in any school need to be responsible stewards realizing that their tenure is relatively short term. Leaders need to adopt a mindset that they need to leave any school they lead in a better state than when they found it. The custodial aspects of school leadership are significant. Any decisions taken will have potentially long-term consequences for the future. Many school leaders have inherited schools that are operating well but others have found the direct opposite. Due to the direct impact of poor leadership, some schools are broken characterized by such characteristics as low levels of trust, psychological unsafe work environment and the misuse of scarce resources on questionable activities. James Kerr (2013, p. 179) evokes us as leaders to 'Be a Good Ancestor – we are the stewards of our organisations, the caretakers of our own lineage'. Such a responsibility is a privilege, honour and weight that bear on any leader.

Realistically, a school leader's legacy will be carried in the heart, heads and hands of others – students, teachers, parents and community members. In shaping a legacy sometimes leaders will face opposition and adversarial circumstances that will need to be engaged with, confronted and removed in the spirit of foreseen broad benefit. School leaders will need to act with courage and sometimes move through the 'storm' and perhaps uncharted waters with self-belief typified by humility, compassion and a desire to contribute to the common good.

Leadership and legacy are intertwined concepts that define the trajectory of individuals, organizations and indeed societies. While leadership is an active process of guiding, enabling, influencing, mobilizing and inspiring others towards common goals and aspirations, legacy is the enduring impact left behind, an imprint that transcends time and continues to shape the future. Together, they form a powerful narrative about purpose, influence and the long-term consequences of leadership actions.

Becoming a leader is an ongoing journey of self-reflection and development. School leaders need to have selfish and generous intent when leading. Selfish intent is about being committed to lifelong learning to be the best version of themselves when leading a school. They also need to act with generous intent – continually refining professional practices to enable their leadership to have a greater contribution and impact.

A leader is 'a pilgrim, not one who has "arrived" at some idealized state of perfection' (Lowney, 2003).

FOR REFLECTION AND DISCUSSION

1. What questions to lead by do you use to reflect on your formation as a school leader?
2. Using the key questions posed in this chapter, write down your key values and beliefs about your role as a school leader. Now, complete the following *short leadership credo/personal vision* statement:

   I do this ...

   Because I hope to ....

   Share your credo with colleagues and invite their feedback. How did they react?
3. Reflect on this *quote from the late Pope Francis* in the context of your work as a school leader:

   'Fast from selfishness and be compassionate to others'.

What does compassionate mean for you as a school leader? Why is it important in enabling a positive school culture and climate?

4. Write down or draw using an image, the people who make up your *Personal Board of Directors*.
5. When you visit a new school or look around at one you are working in, study the building name plates, read a school magazine from a few years ago and other artefacts. Why? Such artefacts are the 'eyes to the soul' of the school and the contribution made by others to the present school culture. What do you notice and observe?
6. Reflect on the importance of *professional trust* in school leadership and the connection to school culture and climate. What are the key behaviours and practices that school leaders enable greater or positive levels of trust in a school?
7. Creating a meaningful *legacy* requires a school leader to be a *responsible steward*. What do you want your legacy to be?

KEY IDEAS

- School leadership is a significant variable in the quality of any school's culture and climate.
- Key questions for all school leaders to consistently ponder about school culture (Deal & Peterson, 2016, Eastwood, 2022).
- Leadership self-awareness and a commitment to ongoing to personal learning are fundamental to enhancing a school's culture and climate.
- All leaders are imperfect and therefore need to continually refine and reflect on their practices. A series of questions can act as a prompt and a framework for this to occur.
- All leaders should develop a leadership credo – a statement of any leader's purpose of 'why?'
- The development of a Personal Board of Directors can assist a school leader navigate the complexity and challenges of their role.

- It is important to understand what others desire and expect from leaders – hope, compassion, trust and stability.
- School leaders are temporary custodians of the school they are entrusted to lead. They need to be responsible stewards and develop diverse, shared approaches to leadership.

REFERENCES

Australian Council of Education Research. (2023). *National school improvement tool*. ACER.

Bennis, W. (2014, July). Leadership excellence essentials. *HR.com*. https://www.hr.com

Browning, P. (2014). *The importance of trust and how to get it – Compelling leadership*. Centre for Research Innovation & Future Development, Apple Books.

Bushe, G. R. (2013). *Appreciative inquiry: Theory and critique*. Jossey-Bass.

Collins, J., & Porras, J. (1994). *Built to last: Successful habits of visionary companies*. Harper Business.

Deal, T. E., & Peterson, K. D. (2016). *Shaping school culture: The heart of leadership*. John Wiley &Sons.

De Botton, A. (2019). *The school of life – An emotional education*. Penguin Random Books.

Dewey, J. (1910). *How we think* (1st ed.). D.C. Heath & Co..

Dobrygowski. (2016, May 30). *There is one key trait that all great leaders share*. World Economic Forum.

Eastwood, O. (2022). *Belonging: Unlock your potential with the ancient code of togetherness*. Quercus Publishing.

Gallup. (2025). *Global leadership report: What followers want*. World Governments Summit.

George, B., Sims, P., McLean, A., & Mayer, D. (2007, February). Discovering your authentic leadership. *Harvard Business Review*.

Goffee, R., & Jones, G. (2006). *Why should anyone be led by you? What it takes to be an authentic leader*. Harvard Business School Press.

Grant, A. (2023). *Hidden potential: The science of achieving greater things*. Random House Large Print.

Hart, N. (2022). *Creating a strong culture and positive climate in schools – Building knowledge to bring about improvement*. Routledge.

Heifetz, R. A., & Laurie, D. L. (2001, December). Managing people: The work of leadership. *Harvard Business Review*.

Hewlin, P. F., Dumas, T. L., & Burnett, M. F. (2015). To thine own self be true? Facades of conformity, values incongruence, and the moderating impact of leader integrity. *Academy of Management Journal*, *60*(1), 178–199.

Hull, J., & Moore, M. (2025, July). 3 Essential self-care habits for compassionate leadership. *Big Think Business*. https://www.bigthink.com/business.

Kegan, R., & Lahey, L. (2016). *The immunity to change approach*. Harvard Graduate School of Education.

Kerr, J. (2013). *Legacy*. Constable.

Lowney, C. (2003). *Heroic leadership – Leadership principles for lasting success*. Loyola Press.

Maister, D. H., Galford, R., & Green, C. (2001). *The trusted advisor*. Simon & Schuster.

Munby, S., & Bretherton, M. (2022). *Imperfect leadership in action*. Crown House Publishing.

Nicholsen, N. (2013). *The "I" of leadership: Strategies for seeing, being and doing*. Jossey-Bass.

OECD. (2015). *G20/OECD principles of corporate governance*. OECD Publishing.

O'Keeffe, A. (2023). *First leaders*. Roundtable Press.

Parks, S. D. (2005). *Leadership can be taught: A bold approach for a complex world*. Harvard University Press.

Rath, T., & Conchie, B. (2008). *Strengths-based leadership: Great leaders, teams, and why people follow*. Gallup Press.

Seppälä, E., & Cameron, K. (2015, December 2). Proof that positive work cultures are more productive. Harvard Business Review.

Thacker, J. L., & McInerney, W. D. (1992). Changing academic culture to improve student achievement in the elementary schools. *ERS Spectrum, 10*(4), 18–23.

The Australian Professional Standard for Principals-Professional Profiles. (2020). *Australian professional standard for principals: Professional profiles.*

The Centre for Creative Leadership. (2025, January 2). *The 16 most-needed leadership competencies.* [online]. www.ccl.org

Westfall, C. (2019, June 20). *Leadership development is a $366 billion industry: Here's why most programs don't work.* https://www.forbes.com/sites/chriswestfall/2019/05/development-why-most-programs-don't work

5

ADAPTIVE LEADERSHIP: THE ESSENCE OF BUILDING POSITIVE SCHOOL CULTURES

Nurturing, renewing, developing and sustaining a positive school culture requires an adaptive approach to leadership characterized by a leadership mindset that values new learning and innovation, and involves new patterns of behaviour within a school (Heifetz et al., 2009). Cultural change in any school involves deeply held values, beliefs, and professional practices and behaviours. Moreover, many of the challenges or developmental opportunities facing schools are complex and not going to be resolved solely by technical 'solutions' using current knowledge and professional practices. The purpose of this chapter is to provide school leaders with perspectives, tools and pragmatic insights drawn from adaptive leadership theory and practice that could be used to assist school leaders to create school cultures that are connected, protected and respected.

So, what in essence is adaptive leadership? Adaptive leadership is the practice of mobilizing people to respond to the toughest challenges that any organization faces to thrive. Such an approach to leadership is readily applicable to the challenges of establishing and enabling a flourishing school culture. This will be explored in later parts of this chapter.

The term 'adaptive leadership' was coined by Harvard Professor, Ronald Heifetz. He articulated five strategic principles that inform an adaptive approach to leadership. These are (1) diagnosing the system, (2) manage distress, (3) identify distractions, (4) delegate effectively and (5) encourage challenge. C. Brown (2025) in his article, 'The Art of War Joint Competency, Clausewitz and Adaptive Leadership – Old Wine in New Bottles?', argues that many of these principles can be linked with the writings of a Prussian army officer of the 1800s, Carl von Clauswitz, for example, listening to dissenting voices and fostering others as agents of change.

Leading using an adaptive orientation and mindset requires certain capabilities and pre-dispositions. What are these? Heifetz et al. (2009) suggest that there are at least four pre-conditions that leaders need to display and consider adopting such an approach to leadership and engaging in the associated work:

1. *Get rid of the broken system's illusion:* There is no such thing as a broken system and any leader who premises their actions on such a basis is perpetuating a mythology. Any system such as a school is operating the way it is because the individuals want it that way. There is no such thing as a dysfunctional organization because every organization is perfectly aligned to achieve the outcomes it currently obtains. In accepting this premise, a leader's crucial role is to facilitate and mobilize people through the enacted disruption brought about by adaptive work.
2. *Learn to live in disequilibrium*: In undertaking adaptive work, a leader is creating dissonance, disturbing established, hegemonic organizational ways of doing and being. Any leader will need to demonstrate the capability to manage this discordant period, decide through discernment what needs to be retained and equally, what is expendable. At an individual level, every leader needs to manage themselves in such turbid times and to assist people to manage the discomfort they may be experiencing.
3. *Engage above and below the neck:* As discussed in Chapter 4, leaders will require courage to address with the requisite mix of will and skill to address adaptive challenges. Courage requires heart, mind, spirit, and guts.

4. *Connect to purpose*: In an earlier chapter, we explored the importance of pivoting back to a leader's purpose, or their personal, why? In the words of Friedrich Nietzsche, 'he who has a why can bear almost any how'. The expression of a leader's personal credo must have a connection to a broader purpose. Heifetz et al. (2009) note that it makes no sense to engage in the practice of leadership unless it is on behalf of some larger purpose that a leader finds compelling.

What's the discernable difference between a technical challenge and an adaptive one? A technical challenge requires the straightforward application of expertise to respond to or solve the presenting problem. For example, school leaders can draw stated policies, guidelines and expectations about how to respond to common or regularly occurring issues such as employee performance and child safeguarding. In some school settings, just establishing and implementing these technical provisions is the adaptive work. An adaptive challenge is arguably much more complex because it necessitates influencing other people's values, habits, practices and priorities. Williams (2025) suggests that such challenges also require the orchestration of deep learning, sustaining some losses to enable progress to occur, getting people to face aspects of their reality they don't wish to face, the stimulation and moderation of mild conflict, the engagement with multiple groups and factions and forces, taking time and invite creativity, innovation and experimentation. School leaders must contend with such problems or puzzles of practice as an ongoing part of leading a school. These problems or puzzles are persistent – they are not one off but recur; shaped by the context of each school; are material to the professional practices and overall improvement of a school; and will require personal commitment of the behalf of an individual.

Heifetz et al. (2009) suggest that there are four adaptive challenge archetypes that recur in most organizations. Archetype one is the gap between espoused values and behaviours. For example, in a school's mission statement there is great emphasis on pastoral care of students, but students have a very negative reality typified by widespread bullying and a lack of intervention and support by school staff. In any organization, leaders must adopt a mantra of behaving our way into the change we want or the shared aspirations desired. Such a discernable difference between espoused values and behaviours gives rise to shadow and potentially, toxic cultures. The second of the archetypes is competing commitments. In an individual's life or any organization such as school there will always be a range of competing commitments that sometimes come into conflict. Friction can be caused, for example, by a contest for financial resources and the priority to be given to certain whole school initiatives. The third of these archetypes is described as speaking the unspeakable. In essence, this relates to the duality of conversations that are ongoing in any organization and within each of us as individuals. Surfacing unspoken conversations will enhance the effectiveness of responding to adaptive challenges. The final archetype is work avoidance. In every organization people have well-developed approaches such as diverting attention and displaced responsibility to protect themselves from facing the discomfort that comes within adaptive challenges. For example, in a schooling context, blaming lower-grade teachers for failing to teach core concepts is required by students to experience success with their current teacher in a primary school.

Williams (2005) provides a useful framework for leaders to examine the types of adaptive challenge(s) that need to be addressed to enable a better improved organizational state and culture:

1. *The activist challenge*: The group or a faction of the group refuses to face some element of reality that might improve the people's quality of life or institutional performance. In a school, this can be seen when teachers are not prepared to adopt new ways of behaviour management or specific approaches to assessment of student work.
2. *The development challenge*: The group can make significant improvements to its quality of life and organizational performance if latent abilities (assets) become effective. In schools, leaders identify and invite people with under-utilized expertise and wisdom to be part of engage in shaping the next set of strategic directions for a school community.
3. *The transition challenge*: There is the possibility of great gains if the group can transition its current value to a new value

set. Leaders regularly face this challenge and opportunity in schools in a myriad of ways. For example, a typical circumstance is about developing school-based teacher professional learning communities which require sharing and collaborating around student performance and teaching practice.

4. *The maintenance challenge*: The 'terrain' is such that the group cannot improve its lot even if it develops the full extent of its latent assets. An interpretation of the dynamic of this challenge is that sometimes in a school or educational system the main priority is to bring a sense of calm and stability for a period to allow leaders to consider the next phase of work.
5. *The creative challenge*: A combination of events presents an unusual opportunity that, if the group can break routine activity long enough to exploit it, might lead to a major and permanent new benefit. In the context of schools and educational systems, leaders who see and opportunity to partner with a university or provider to deliver enhanced pathways for young people, diversifying and extending educational provision into the early childhood sector and providing access to schooling through a hybrid model for trauma impacted students through a combination of support responses.
6. *The crisis challenge*: The group faces a potentially explosive situation that threatens the life of the group or some aspects of the prevailing order. There are countless examples of specific incidents or sustainable endemic aspects of the culture of some schools or systems of schools that through discovery can present real potential for significant reputation harm, for example, failure of school system governing bodies to oversight and attend to required regulatory compliance; widespread historical cases of sexual molestation and abuse of students that require repatriation; and the failure to respond to known corrupt use of public resources for private purposes.

A challenge may have characteristics as one of the previous types of challenges but typically in context can have multiple dimensions, complexities and therefore challenges. For example, a crisis challenge can be caused by or have a connection or link to a developmental dimension.

Leaders can use the above as a meta framework and tool to diagnose and focus their adaptive leadership efforts. The practice of adaptive leadership consists of four groups of interconnected activities:

(1) diagnosis of the system;
(2) mobilization of the system;
(3) understanding of self as a system; and
(4) deployment of self.

One of the most common errors by leaders is a failure to take enough time to diagnose the nature of the adaptive challenge; the political landscape; the presenting culture norms, behaviours and the current capabilities to enable collective action. Leaders, as stated in previous chapters, need to be 'first-class noticers' – observing, monitoring and reflecting constantly about the ways of doing things around a school. In this diagnostic stage it is important for leaders to analyse the technical and adaptive aspects of the work to be undertaken along with the current state of the culture – the cultural forces and norms that affirm the status quo; the nuances of relationships – the 'tribes', factions, loyalties and alliances that exist and to name any potential or implied loss that any adaptation will incur.

As discussed in previous chapters, the establishment, monitoring, nuance and fostering of a positive school culture is never complete. It is ongoing and a primary focus for any school leader. What are some of the pre-conditions or cultural features that a leader can promulgate within a school that enable adaptation and a school culture that is dynamic and positive.

Heifetz et al. (2009) suggest that there are five distinguishing characteristics of an adaptive culture: (1) elephants in the room are named; (2) responsibility for the organization's future is shared; (3) independent judgement is expected; (4) leadership capacity is developed; and (5) reflection and continuous learning are institutionalized. Such features are essential to the creation of a connected, protected and respected school culture. In chapters of this book, we have explored and affirmed each of these dimensions in leading cultural change.

School leaders must have the capability of tangling with organizational temple cats like the metaphor of naming the elephants in the room. Connected, protected and respected school cultures are ones in which all voices are heard and respected. Moreover, the ways of doing and being 'around here' are open to question, refinement and challenge without fear, favour and psychological harm. The leadership and responsibility for the culture of a school is a shared one. Leaders are the temporary custodians and stewardship of any school for a period. In enabling a shared sense of ownership for any school's future there is greater potential for responsiveness and tapering to emerging circumstances. Any school will be potentially better able to respond to such challenges if its staff do not expect the school leadership team and formal leaders to have all the answers.

In a healthy school culture, agency, independent thinking and perspectives are nurtured and respected. In keeping with the spirit of shared responsibility and ownership, identifying and growing leadership density is of profound importance to sustain and enliven a quality, adaptable school culture.

In schools that thrive, reflection and learning at an individual, team and whole school level are evident. Learning is a part of cultural practice of the school. Leaders are deliberate and intentional about supporting people to acquire the requisite capabilities to experience success in their work. Leaders must be adept in moving between the metaphorical 'dance floor', the everyday activity of a school to 'the balcony', a position of space that allows them to observe patterns that are occurring rather than being swept up by them. Williams (2025) notes that leaders need to 'zoom in' and 'zoom out' during the diagnostic phase to gain an understanding of what is happening on the ground while also scanning the broader environment for emerging patterns and trends that could impact this work. Harvey et al. (2025) in their article, 'New Research on the Link Between Learning and Innovation', suggest that there are four essential ways every leadership team should be learning: reflexive-assessing strategies, revisiting goals and discussing challenges; experimental-brainstorming, prototyping and testing new ideas; contextual-scanning the environment for trends, signals, shifts and vicarious – drawing lessons from others who have done similar work. The adoption of such a deliberate approach to learning teams is a much better place to be more proactive and positioned to engage in strategic decision-making and consider innovative practices. The three fields of knowledge of networked learning developed by the National College of School Leadership (2003) are a useful tool to additional or supplementary deploy in the diagnosis phase of adaptive work. The model invites practitioners to consider: (a) what we (they) know? – the knowledge of those involved – what practitioners know; (b) what is known? – the knowledge from theory, research and best practice; and (c) new knowledge – the new knowledge that we (they) can create together through collaborative work.

School leaders in undertaking adaptive work should in the initial or diagnostic phase undertake a pragmatic assessment of the current state of its capacity and culture against the above key characteristics that make any organization adaptive.

The next stage of enabling adaptive work is how then does a school leadership group mobilize its people and resources within their distinctive context to enable a coherent, precise and appropriate response. Again in this phase it is necessary to be ascertaining and enabling the critical dimensions of an adaptive culture discussed previously – elephants in the room or temple cats are named; there is a sense of collective ownership or stewardship of the organization; shared leadership is in evidence; invest in the formation is deliberate; independent judgement and insights are valued and ongoing learning along with reflective practices are present in the everyday operational cycle of the school. This is a continuous process and core requirement of any leadership team entrusted with the governance of a school. In addition to the tendering of an adaptive culture, Heifetz et al. (2009) note that based on their diagnosis leaders need to make multiple and diverse range of interpretations; design effective interventions; act politically; and to orchestrate conflict. In this intervention phase, leaders need to remember to take a balcony view; create a holding environment that allows time, opinion and diverse viewpoints to be expressed; the heat to be turned up or down when ideas are being challenged or conversely ignored. In applying this approach to leadership, it is useful to remember the mantras that the work to be undertaken needs to be kept at the centre of all deliberations and that the work should be handed back to the people because ultimately, the people need to own it.

Williams (2025) describes a five-A intervention and mobilization approach to this phase of engaging with an adaptive challenge(s) (see Table 5).

Table 5. The Five-A Process for Intervention and Mobilization.

Processes	Technical	Adaptive
ASPIRATION	• Vision statement • Destination, goal • Top down/given	Imagination + bold + reality testing Higher purpose (adds value) What's at stake? What is progress?
ANALYSIS	• 'I already know' • Spotlight on the box/ expert/authority • Focus on the technical data and technical solutions	Spotlight on the adaptive challenge versus technical challenge Keep 'the work' at the centre What is going on in the background? Work avoidance dynamics Who can I partner with?
AGREEMENT	• Defer to authority • Focus on compliance • Chimpanzee politics, the alpha process	Bring background concerns to the foreground Focus on enrolment and partnership Reduce 'alpha process' and chimp politics
ACTION	• Follow the boss • Reduce disequilibrium • Operate within boundary (silos and tribes) • Play it safe	Facilitate leadership conversations Manage intensity of 'disequilibrium' Help people work at the boundaries Address work avoidance
ASSESSMENT	• KPI's • Accountability • Blame	Are we making real progress? Learn from breakdowns and failures My leadership – what am I learning?

Source: www.leaderscompass.com

It is important that leaders undertake an initial assessment of the current and aspired states or the intended aspiration(s) are clarified: In the agreement phase, being deliberate about the engagement of key stakeholders; the reduction of deference to authority figures; and the use of strategies to move background thinking to the foreground of deliberations. In another chapter of this book, we have explored the importance of leaders having conversational capacity to enable the adaptive process. Conversations are the circulatory system of a school. A critical point to note that when doing adaptive work, current state will never meet aspired state. Leaders should always be open to feedback and learning to refine and re-define current and aspired states. In short, the gap between these two positions will be the adaptive leadership work to be undertaken.

As noted above, the final two aspects of the approach to adaptive leadership relate to the individual or self as a leader – seeing oneself as a system and the deployment of self as a leader in enabling the work to be done. The importance of nurturing self, connecting with purpose, being courageous, inspiring others, self-reflection and awareness have been explored in previous chapters.

One of the dimensions that need to be amplified is the notion of individual identity.

We all have a professional profile and identity typically attached to a role – school principal, leader of curriculum, chief executive officer, deputy principal, area supervisor and so on. In leadership it is important to discern who you are, what you value and what you care about. Such conscious deliberation and contemplation give rise to a leader's why, their purpose. However, all of us have multiple identities, a multiple mix of personal and professional roles we manage as we undertake living our lives.

Our self-representation consists of multiplicity. The contrasting cognitive behaviours we possess are merely because we do not have a singular self-identity that fully governs our thoughts, values and emotions. There are multiple identities inside each one of us. Inside of adopting the view of a person as one whole self, everyone can be considered a range of distinct but related identities (Institute of Managers and Leaders, 2025). This is important to remember when leaders are working with others, considering decisions and preferences that we adopt when responding to problems of practice. We need to acknowledge and leverage multiple identities in our workplaces.

In leadership we must also remember to separate ourselves from self and role. Heifetz and Laurie (2017) in their text, Leadership on the Line, note that the roles we play in our organizations, community and in our private lives are mainly dependent on the expectations of the people we interact with and who surround us. They contend that the self relies on our individual capacity to witness and learn throughout our lives; to refine the core values that orient and inform our decision-making; and whether they conform to expectations.

What does this mean for our leadership practices to enable us to sustain ourselves and enable us to thrive in our roles? To continue to be compassionate, curious, positive and hope-filled in the pursuit of shared aspirations? We need anchors that keep us centred supported by sanctuaries, special places or experiences that take us back to who we are and renew us (after Heifetz & Laurie, 2017).

The most beautiful people we have known are those who have known defeat, known suffering, known struggle, known loss and found their way out of the depths. These people have an appreciation, a sensitivity and an understanding of life that fills them with compassion, gentleness and a deep loving concern. Beautiful people do not just happen (Elizabeth Kubler Ross).

The leadership of adaptive work can be personally taxing requiring resilience and resolve.

School leaders need to have the capability to think and act strategically. City and Curtis (2025) suggest that at the heart of strategic leadership are five interrelated elements: (1) discernment: clarifying what truly matters to fulfil the organization's vision; (2) intentionally nurturing interpersonal connections and social networks; (3) deep knowledge of context and history – understanding the organizational landscape, its patterns and its roots; (4) power awareness – identifying where influence resides and strategically employing it to advance shared goals; and (5) embracing a cycle of thinking big, acting small and learning fast. An adaptive approach provides a methodology, principles and an associated practical set of tactics, tools and strategies to support leaders to focus strategically on school culture.

FOR REFLECTION AND DISCUSSION

1. List down the adaptive leadership challenges you and your school/schooling system face.
2. Related to the above, what is the adaptive work that needs to be done to respond effectively to each one of the named challenges? What are the associated technical and adaptive aspects of these?
3. Use the Williams (2005) adaptive leadership framework to describe the most pressing and critical adaptive challenge you face as a leader in your current role and context.
4. In your context is there any evidence of archetypal adaptive challenges? If so, in what specific ways is this occurring and why?
5. In your schooling system or school, what are the realities that leaders, decision-makers and stakeholders must face to make progress? What is at stake if they are not tackled?
6. Using the 'five-A' process described by Williams (2025) to look at a current adaptive leadership challenge you and your team face. What aspects of need further focus and or refinement?

KEY IDEAS

- There are at least four pre-conditions that leaders need to display and consider when adopting an adaptive approach to leadership: (1) removal of the idea of a broken system; (2) learning to live with disequilibrium; (3) engaging above and below the neck; and (4) connecting and reverting to purpose.
- The difference between a technical and adaptive challenge.
- There are at least four adaptive challenge archetypes according to Heifetz et al. (2009): (1) the gap between espoused values and behaviours; (2) competing commitments; (3) speaking the unspeakable; and (4) work avoidance.
- Williams' (2005) types of adaptive challenges: activist, development, transition, maintenance, creative and crisis.
- Four distinct but interconnected activities of adaptive leadership work: (1) diagnosis of the system; (2) mobilization of the

system; (3) understanding of self as a system; and (4) deployment of self.

- Heifetz et al. (2009) contend that there are five distinguishing characteristics of an adaptive culture: (1) elephants in the room are named; (2) responsibility for the organization's future is shared; (3) independent judgement is expected; (4) leadership capacity is developed and reflection; and (5) continuous learning are institutionalized.
- Four essential ways in which every leadership team should be learning: (1) reflexive; (2) experimental; (3) contextual; and (4) vicarious.
- The three fields of knowledge as the basis for a networked approach to learning.
- Williams' (2025) five-A process for intervention and mobilization – (1) aspiration; (2) analysis; (3) agreement; (4) action; and (5) assessment.
- Multiple professional identities and the importance of cultivating sanctuaries to sustain oneself in leadership.
- City and Curtis (2025) suggest there are five interrelated aspects of thinking strategically as a school leader: (1) discernment; (2) nurturing interpersonal connections and social networks; (3) deep knowledge of context and history; (4) power awareness; and (5) embracing a cycle of thinking big, acting small and learning fast.

REFERENCES

Brown, C. (2025, March 11). The art of war joint competency. Clausewitz and adaptive leadership – Old wine in new bottles? *The Forge*.

Brown, S. (2025, October). Someone's daughter, a child's mother. *Education Matters Secondary Magazine*.

City, J. A., & Curtis, R. E. (2025). *Leading strategically achieving ambitious goals in education*. Harvard University Press.

Harvey, J.-F., Cromwell, J., Johnson, J., & Edmondson, A. (2025, July 14). New research on the link between learning and innovation. *Harvard Business Review.*

Heifetz, R. (1994). *Leadership without easy answers.* Belknap Press, Harvard University Press.

Heifetz, R., Grashow, A., & Linsky, M. (2009). *The practice of adaptive leadership: Tools and tactics for changing your organisation and the world.* Harvard Business Press.

Institute of Managers and Leaders. (2025, June 13). *Australian and New Zealand, leveraging your different identities.*

National College of School Leadership. (2003). *Networked learning – Three fields of knowledge.*

Williams, D. (2005). *Real leadership: Helping people and organizations face their toughest challenges.* Berrett-Koehler.

Williams, D. (2025). *Adaptive leadership in a crazy world.* Masterclass Notes.

6

'TANGLING WITH YOUR TEMPLE CATS': CHALLENGING OUTMODED BEHAVIOURS, NORMS AND PRACTICES AT THE HEART OF LEADING CULTURAL CHANGE

Temple cats? These cats come in many shapes, sizes, forms and colours, and exhibit various behaviours. Some are content to prowl around untamed, others prefer to eat, sleep, yawn and observe the passing parade, while others habitually get ready to catch their next quarry through various dubious and deliberate moves. Welcome to the world of the temple cat, a metaphor for the dynamic reality of any school or indeed organization. 'Temple cats' exist in every organization – they are the policies, procedures, practices and people behaviours that inhibit progress, are never challenged, contribute little, have nothing positive to utter, lack authenticity and are self-serving. Kriegel and Brandt (1996) in their popular text, *Sacred Cows Make the Best Burgers: Developing Change-Driving People and Organisations*, note that these 'temple cats' or 'sacred cows' typically express as outmoded beliefs, assumptions, practices and policies that prevent responsiveness to new opportunities and innovation.

What can we learn from the tale of the Guru's cat?

> When the guru sat down to worship each evening, the ashram cat would get in the way and distract the worshippers. So, he ordered that the cat be tied during evening worship.
>
> After the guru died, the cat continued to be tied during evening worship. And when the cat expired, another cat was brought to the ashram so that it could be duly tied during evening worship.
>
> Centuries later, learned treatises were written by the guru's scholarly disciples on the liturgical significance of tying up a cat while worship is performed.

The story of the guru's cat is an encouragement and an invitation to review what we do habitually and to ask: Why do we do what we do? Why do we say what we say? Why do we use what we use? Is what we're doing still appropriate and beneficial today? Is what we're doing daily still achieving what it was originally intended to do? Or is it perhaps becoming a distraction, clutter, confusion ... another guru's or temple cat?

Leading cultural change involves engaging with the bedrock of a school's culture, those embedded and foundational beliefs that are at its core. Leadership of cultural change is not for faint-hearted leaders, it requires courage, resilience, and a desire to act in the best interests of all. Sometimes leaders are afflicted with condition blindness, accepting or simply not being aware of the temple cats that are embedded in a school as accepted or unchallenged behaviours.

Leading change by its very nature involves others shifting mindsets, challenging assumptions and re-setting culture. It's complex, dynamic, messy and adaptive work, never easy but immensely rewarding. This work as school leaders must be on behalf of realizing the moral purpose of all schools and their leaders, to have all children achieve their potential in safe, caring and supportive school environments. Equally, this can only be achieved with the work and support of adults who also feel connected, protected and respected in any school dynamic.

Where to start is always a conundrum when leading cultural reformation and change? How do you as a leader or leaders of a school start to engage with these temple cats as a realistic aspect of enabling a future, better, better, desired state for the school?

In short, there is no single formula but a range of variable, strategies, approaches and considerations that school leaders need to consider when responding to such challenges, opportunities and realities of the school's context, culture and prevailing climate.

As noted in earlier chapters, school leaders need to be 'contextually literate'. Southworth (2009) explains that being contextually literate involves how the school operates; exploring that mosaic and complexity of relationships that are at play; what values that inform practices, customs; strengths and areas for improvement and the nature of the school community setting. Contextual sensitivity is not only about recognizing such factors but then adopting a forensic approach to how these relate and the current state of these relationships. This is a leadership disposition that will be essential before engaging and enabling form of change.

An immediate consideration for any school leader in leading change is to consider their theory of change, a meta framework that provides a broad outline of how cultural change will be led. It is important that whatever approach is adopted must be owned by the leader, informed by various perspectives and made transparent to increase shared ownership.

A variety of theoretical approaches to leading change abound. These range from Simon Sinek's (2009) Golden Circle Theory focusing on the articulation and communication of the Why, How and the What of change; John Kotter's (1996) Eight-Stage Process of Creating Major Change-establishing a sense of urgency, creating a guiding coalition; developing a vision and strategy, communicating the change vision, empowering broad based action, generating short-term wins, consolidating gains and producing more change and anchoring new approaches in the culture; Kurt Lewin's (1951) three-stage change model of unfreeze, change and refreeze; Senge's (1990) approach consisting of five main and interrelated disciplines of team learning, shared vision, mental models, personal mastery; systems thinking; and Michael Fullan's (2008) six secrets of change – love your employees, connect peers with purpose, capacity building prevails, learning is the work, transparency rules and systems learn.

Arguably, the second and related phase of leading change for any school leader is to develop a 'theory of action', a plan that has a clear pathway that links actions to a preferred set of outcomes

(Argyris & Schon, 1996). Theories of action are practical tools for helping describe and align efforts to achieve positive, purposeful change in a school. Fullan (2008, p. 8) confirms this interplay between theory and action when he notes that leaders need 'theories that travel'. Good leaders are thoughtful managers who use their theory of action to govern what they do while being open to surprises, ideas and new data that informs further action. However, in the reality of a key component of any travel plan in a school context are people who have their own theories of actions. Viviane Robinson's (2018) work, *Reducing Change to Increase Improvement*, notes that school leaders can either bypass teachers' theory of action or engage with these. There are different assumptions and positions by any school leader she suggests will result in either compliance, resistance or adaptation by teachers or a joint resolution to marshal collective attention or not, to an area of school improvement.

Research acknowledges the importance of coherence and coordination of such effort and activities aimed at improving a school:

> *As challenging as it is, when school improvement plans align with strategically identified directions and the focus on long term sustainable solutions, rather than quick fixes, they can lead to substantial improvements in student outcomes. Coherence means that the focus of improvement focused activities is consistent across the school. This requires aligning individual and organisational needs and ensuring the improvement agenda is explicit. (Rogers et al., 2023, p. 2)*

Hallie et al. (2019) provide a useful insight into the factors affecting a school staff's motivation, willingness and capacity to change for change. These are captured in their conceptual model (see Fig. 3).

This research isolates four promising approaches that school leaders can apply to consider and maximize the readiness to connect with their staff to engage positively engage with any proposed change. These are (1) taking a change leadership approach; (2) considering and assessing staff's motivation and capacity to change; (3) the incorporation of feedback into implementation planning; and

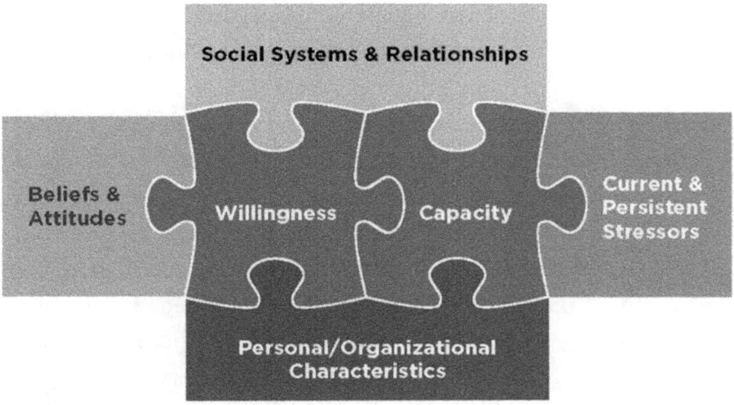

Fig. 3 Conceptual Model for Readiness and Factors Affecting Readiness for Change by Hallie et al. (2019).

(4) regularly reviewing levels of readiness for change. Organizational readiness for change hasn't received the attention it deserves when considering enabling change initiatives (AERO, 2023).

School leaders need to have a deep understanding and knowledge of how schools improve and the associated leadership behaviours, capabilities that are necessary to enable high leverage improvement strategies to have impact. So, what do school leaders pay attention to with the aim of improving a school and, therefore, the ultimate benchmark of improving student learning outcomes. The various interrelated and foundational levers broadly fall into three categories: data, planning and capability.

School leaders consistently access, gather, reflect and use data to inform decision making, areas for collective focus and to support teaching practice. There is compelling research evidence with respect to the effective use of data in enabling and informing an improvement agenda in any school.

In relation to planning, better performing schools are typified by a shared vision, evidence of collaborative practice, clarity of strategic imperatives and a commitment to ongoing feedback, refinement based on transparent processes typically informed by multiple voices – student, staff, parent, community and other contextually relevant perspectives. Viviane Robinson's work on student centred leadership notes that the development and articulation of goals and expectations is one of five high-value leadership practices by any school leader(s) in enabling better outcomes for students.

The other interconnected dimension is that of capability. Arguably, this is the most crucial aspect that needs to be present to enable desired, exposed change and the inevitable 'temple cats' to be tangled with. Leadership is at the core of this work characterized by behaviours that manifest in ways of doing things 'around here'. There is evidence of shared leadership, high levels of trust, role clarity, focus on team development, a commitment to organizational learning, a strong sense of connection and purpose by staff, respect and shared set of high expectations for everyone.

Any organization like a school exists for a purpose, to do something, what it hopes to achieve. All the activities, including the behaviour of its people, should contribute to achieving its purpose. The Australian Institute of Company Directors (2019) provides a useful framework for leaders to regularly consider in relation to an organization purpose and any intended change strategy: Why does this organization (school) exist? What does this organization (school) do? Who does this organization (school) benefit? How does this organization (school) achieve its goals? And what does success look like for this organization (school)? An ongoing challenge for school leaders is to continue to connect and align stakeholders to its purpose and articulated strategy in keeping with its espoused values. The challenge of alignment for any school leader is that it is never a static state – it needs constant attention, nurturing and focus and akin to herding cats. A school leader's aspiration should be to endeavour to get a critical mass of stakeholders and factional groups broadly enrolled in the direction of the school. It is pure folly to suggest that all individuals will at any time, and at the same time, be on board with the change agenda of the institution.

The intersection of any change with the dynamic, ecosystem of any school will always require hypersensitivity and focus by a leader. When we have significant and discernable differences between individual perspectives, values and priorities and those of the collective, this provides fertile grounds for metaphorical 'temple cats' archetype behaviour to flourish.

Leading change is a necessary practice and associated set of behaviours for any school leader. However, many fear the dance or the 'tangle' with the annoying, negative and sometimes aggressive people – those who won't or can't see the value of a proposed change; others who have a cause or long held intractable positions based on various ideologies; staff members who have fallen out of love with teaching and have become disenchanted and even a number who are 'immune to change' (Kegan & Lahey, 2009). However, as humans overtime, we have adapted, adopted, pivoted and evolved, so we can and do change.

So, what can leaders do that will enable them to lead change for the better? At the heart of leading change are people and our basic 'human instincts'. Such a contention and statement may not be profound but leading change is both simple and complex given that individuals and their behaviours are at play. O'Keeffe (2011) has developed a useful framework, shown in Table 6, that describes the hardwired human instincts that we all have and exhibit.

He contends that organizational life is made harder than it needs to be because leadership practices don't account for and are contrary to such instincts. According to O'Keeffe (2009) leading change typifies this. The key instinct that needs to be addressed is 'loss aversion'. Humans are significantly more motivated about a particular change initiative if they perceive gain in some form and vice versa. In a schooling context, examples of this could be better

Table 6. Leader Behaviour Framework.

Thinking and Feeling – How Humans Think and Feel	
Emotions before reason	Humans trust their emotional instincts above all else and use emotions as their first screen for all information received. We hear negative news first and loudest.
First impressions to classify	Humans quickly classify people, situations and experiences into categories (good or bad, in or out) based on first impressions and 'gut feelings', rather than engage in time-consuming analysis.
Loss aversion	Humans seek to avoid loss and risky situations but fight frantically when feeling threatened. We explore and are curious about the world around us when we feel safe.

(Continued)

Table 6. (Continued)

Gossip	Humans groom through social chitchat. We are hardwired to seek and share information. We share information with others we like and use it to build alliances. We love to tell and hear stories.
Empathy and mind reading	Humans utilize empathy and mind reading to build relationships, be friendly and gather information. We seek to read other people's thoughts and emotions from their face.
Confidence before realism	Humans radiate confidence to move forward in the world, often denying what is realistic. We allow confidence to conquer realism to get what we want.
Contest and display	Humans seek to impress others and to demonstrate their worth as a means to gain advantages. We spend inordinate amounts of time and energy making ourselves look good in various ways.
Social Living – How Humans Live	
Social belonging	Humans desire strong bonds within family-sized groups of around 7 people and a sense of belonging in clans of up to 150.
Hierarchy and status	Humans seek superiority or security in hierarchical systems. We seek status symbols, recognition and elevation within the hierarchy.

Source: Nicholson (1998, 2000).

teaching conditions and more resourcing support. Heifetz amplifies this when he states that with innovation leaders should always remember that someone's innovation represents another person's loss, for example, changing a long-term year-level teacher, re-structuring the school's executive team or adopting a new whole school approach to assessment of writing. David Rock (2009) in his book *Your Brain at Work* outlined the SCARF model that provides a useful into how social connection between people and their workplace can be viewed:

Status: Relates to how we perceive our position in relation to others we have a relationship with such as our boss, peers, direct reports. Status can be viewed as the drive we have to stand out from the crowd, we are acknowledged for our work and seen to be perhaps an acknowledged thought leader or voice by others in field of work.

Certainty: Humans naturally like to know what's going on. We like to understand our surroundings. At work, we feel threats to our certainty when our roles or responsibilities aren't totally clear and when meetings start to go long, without any clear end in sight.

Autonomy: When leaders involve themselves with every little detail of their team members' work, they risk creating threats to those people's autonomy. (This is why micromanaging feels so offensive.) However, when leaders give employees the time and space to do their work, unfettered by interruptions, they send a much more rewarding signal that they trust and value the person's ability to get things done.

Relatedness: Relatedness is the sense that we belong – that we're in the in-group. Leaders can use language such as 'we' and 'us' to promote that feeling, instead of language like 'you', 'me' and 'they', which signals a clear boundary between groups. Indeed, political research finds that the collective pronouns predict the chance of a politician getting elected.

Fairness: Lastly, humans innately feel a sense of equity and equality in social interactions. We prefer what's justified over what's tilted in one party's favour.

Finding and unlocking what motivates staff is one of the perennial challenges for any school leader. Daniel Pink's (2009) work on motivation provides another useful framework and equation for consideration:

Autonomy + Mastery + Purpose = Motivation

People in the workplace desire agency have the appropriate set of skills, competencies to do their role, feel supported, have the time to do the required work, can draw on relative experience, have purpose and are connected to a higher or greater good. School leaders can draw on Pink's meta framework to provide authentic opportunities for each of these aspects of motivation to be experienced.

Moreover, school leaders need to check free themselves from hegemonic mindsets and language that is typically conveyed with such statements as 'we need to get everyone on board' or that metaphoric 'bus'. School leaders will constantly wrestle with this dynamic in leading culture change.

LEARNING IS THE WORK

Arguably, one of the critical characteristics of a thriving school culture is the presence of a culture of learning. Fullan (2008) notes that 'learning is the work' which is typified by deliberate approach to engage staff in exploring the knowledge and capabilities required to respond to the challenges of improvement and coherence. Effective principals facilitate the establishment of quality trusting, professional relationships across any school community. They ensure that there is a dual focus on student and staff learning and care underpinned by the desire and commitment to ongoing improvement (van der Kleij et al., 2023). Sadly, despite the importance of learning as a key enabler of change in a school and organizations it is 'conspicuous by its absence' in prevailing approaches to organizational design and change (Conigrave, 2022). Typically, organizations are geared towards implementation and delivery of new ideas, innovation and practices but fail to focus on the learning required to enable the aspired change. Kegan (1994) cited in Conigrave (2022) notes that 'organisations today are designed for delivery not development'.

The conditions for learning in situ should be nurtured to enable optimal opportunities for professional learning. The degree to which a school establishes these will greatly depend on its culture – the beliefs, values, attitude, knowledge and skills of its teachers and leaders. Effective school leaders understand the importance of professional learning as a key part of a broader strategy for school improvement.

Effective schools are learning communities that have at their core a culture of collaboration and collective efficacy typified by a desire for improvement in teaching practices and student outcomes.

School leaders need to adopt a deliberate approach to the establishment of the various mechanisms to enable collaboration and maximize engagement. The promotion of teamwork and the nurturing of high performing teams is a necessary strategy to promulgate learning culture.

It should be remembered that high performing teams do not occur naturally; they are consciously and systematically built and designed by leaders in collaboration with their workforce.

What makes a high performing team? An extraordinary amount of research, opinion and leadership development activity has and continues to focus on this question.

In 2017, Google conducted an extensive research study on their teams and organizational teamwork. The study noted the dynamics of effective teams as:

1. *Psychological safety*: team members feel safe to take risks and be vulnerable in front of each other.
2. *Dependability*: team members get things done on time and meet Google's high bar for excellence.
3. *Structure and clarity*: team members have clear roles, plans and goals.
4. *Meaning*: work personally is important to team members.
5. *Impact*: team members think their work matters and creates change.

These findings and characteristics align with other studies of note on high performing workplace teams.

Wageman et al. (2008) in their extensive study of senior leadership teams noted that there are six conditions for senior leadership team effectiveness, three 'essentials' and the other three 'enablers'. The 'essentials' are creating a real team rather than one in name only; developing a clear and compelling purpose; and having team members who have the right mix of skills, experience and capabilities (Wageman et al., 2008, p. 15). The enablers for successful teamwork and ongoing development are team coaching, the generation of a supportive context and a solid structure (Wageman et al., 2008, p. 14).

Lencioni's (2002) seminal work on the five dysfunctions of a team affirms and aligns with the identified team effectiveness characteristics; absence of trust, fear of conflict, lack of commitment, avoidance of accountability and inattention to results.

The GRPI model of team effectiveness suggests that there are four building blocks that enable teams to achieve a high level of performance: Goals – collective vision, aligned objectives and reliable strategy; Roles – clearly defined roles, accountabilities and clear boundaries; Processes – effective processes that support decision-making, planning and resources, conflict resolution, communication; and Interpersonal relationships – positive and support environment, co-operative team behaviours, openness, honesty and trust and innovation and risk taking (adapted from Rubin et al., 1977).

The seminal work of Tuckman (1965) reminds all leaders that any team goes through several discrete and discernible of development: forming, storming, norming, performing and ultimately adjourning. Moreover, any team to reach a high level of performance cannot skip or miss a stage of development. Any team is a constantly changing dynamic due to factors such as member turnover, the impact of unforeseen emergent matters and change of leadership.

At the heart of teamwork and collaboration is professional trust. Maister et al. (2001) describe the concept in the term of an equation with four 'objective' variables:

Credibility – others can trust the advice, information provided by an individual.

Reliability – this relates to an individual actions – they are seen to be dependable and reliable.

Intimacy – other share or entrust information with others confident that it won't be shared to a wider audience.

Self-orientation – refers to where the focus or motivation of an individual is personal or for the common good.

In sustaining and maturing collaborative practices such as teamwork one of the ongoing challenges for school leaders is to enable peer accountability – the willingness of team members to hold each other to account for commitments. This according to Lencioni

(2002) is most effective because it doesn't come or depend on a line manager only but is an acceptance by a team of the reciprocity of their actions, behaviours and work. High performing teams and collaborative work thrive in a school cultures in which individuals connected, protected and respected. Specifically, staff are connected to a common purpose, share vulnerability, feel psychologically safe.

Leading cultural change can sometimes be viewed as like the metaphor of 'making the elephant dance'. The 'elephant' being the school or organization that is slow to move and is unwieldy and the 'dance' representing its ability to be dynamic and adaptable. A reality facing any school leader is to understand that tangling with temple cats is an inevitable aspect of enabling the 'dance' to be choreographed.

FOR REFLECTION AND DISCUSSION

1. In your school context list down the 'temple cats' or 'guru's cats' that you believe exist? Discuss with your colleagues the reasons why they exist and how should they be tangled with?
2. How do you as a leader spot or identify a 'temple cat'?
3. What steps or approaches should school leaders adopt to guard against condition blindness?
4. What factors does a leader need to focus on to be contextually literate?
5. What is your approach to leading change? What mindsets, beliefs and values inform this?
6. Discuss, deliberate and debate with school leaders your theory of change and action.
7. How do you engage staff to optimize the potential of any change initiative designed to improve school culture?
8. Reflect on your experiences with change initiatives. Recount a time in a school when a change was successfully implemented and conversely, when it was unsuccessful. What factors continued to the success or failure of the initiative?
9. Reflect upon your school's learning strategy. What are its components? In what areas or aspects could it be improved and or refined?

10. What is the level of teamwork and collaboration at your school. Reflecting upon the various perspectives on high performing teams, what could be further enhanced?
11. Discuss the ideas of 'loss aversion' and 'someone's innovation represents another person's loss' in your school context.
12. Professional trust is at the heart of positive school cultures. Reflect upon the factors that determine positive and negative levels you have experienced in schools.

KEY IDEAS

- 'Temple cats' is a metaphor to describe some of the outmoded mindsets, beliefs, policies and practices that inhibit responsiveness, adaptation and innovation in school culture.
- Leading sustainable cultural change involves 'tangling with', disturbing and disrupting these 'temple cats'.
- Leading cultural change requires school leaders to have a meta-strategy that has a theory of change and a theory of action.
- The key readiness factors for any school leader to consider in enacting change: adopting a change leadership approach; considering and assessing degrees and levels of staff motivation; planning and feedback; and an overall judgement about a collective readiness for change.
- There are typically three distinct but interconnected levers for school improvement – data, planning and capability.
- Leading any form of change means and mastering human instincts.

High performing teams and collaboration are enabled by a common set of leadership practices and approaches. These include peer accountability, clarity of roles, productive conflict and professional trust.

- A crucial component of a positive, thriving school culture is a commitment to learning.

REFERENCES

Argyris, C., & Schon, D. (1996). *Organizational learning: A theory of action perspective*. Addison Wesley.

Australian Education Research Organisation (AERO). (2023). *Identifying and addressing implementation enablers and barriers*. edresearch.edu.au

Australian Institute of Company Directors. (2019, January 30). *Principle 1: Purpose and strategy*. www.aicd.com.au

Conigrave, N. (2022, October). *Leadership as a learning activity*. CSE Leading Education Series #13. Centre for Strategic Education.

Fullan, M. (2008). *The six secrets of change: What the best leaders do to help their organisations survive and thrive*. Jossey-Bass.

Hallie, T., Partika, A., & Nagle, K. (2019). *Measuring readiness for change in early care and education* [OPRE Report #2019-63]. Office of Planning, Research and Evaluation. Administration for Children and Families, U.S. Department of Health and Human Services.

Kegan, R., & Lahey, L. (2009). *Immunity to change: How to overcome it and unlock potential in yourself and your organization*. Harvard Business Review Press.

Kotter, J. P. (1996). *Leading change*. Harvard Business School Press.

Kriegel, R., & Brandt, D. (1996). *Sacred cows make the best burgers: Paradigm-busting strategies for developing change – Ready people and organisations*. Harper Business.

Lencioni, P. (2002). *The five dysfunctions of a team. A leadership fable*. Jossey-Bass.

Lewin, K. (1951). *Field theory in social science*. Harper Brothers.

Maister, D., Green, C. H., & Galford, R. M. (2001). *The trusted advisor*. Free Press.

Nicholson, N. (1998, July). How hardwired is human behaviour? *Harvard Business Review*, 76(4), 134–147.

Nicholson, N. (2000). *Managing the human animal*. Texere Publishing.

O'Keeffe, A. (2009, June). *Basic instincts* (pp. 36–37). AFR. Boss.com.au

O'Keeffe, A. (2011). *Hardwired humans*. Roundtable Press.

Pink, D. (2009). *Drive: The surprising truth about what motivates us*. Riverhead Books.

Robinson, V. (2018). *Reduce change to increase improvement*. Corwin.

Rock, D. (2009). *Your brain at work: Strategies for overcoming distraction, regaining focus, and working smarter all day long*. HarperCollins.

Rogers, C, Van der Kleji, F., & Taylor-Guy, P. (2023). *School improvement tool: A summary of the underpinning research*. Australian Council of Educational Research. http://doi.org/10.37517/978-1-74286-691-8

Rubin, I. M., Plovnick, M. S., & Fry, R. E. (1977). *Task orientated team development*. McGraw Hill.

Senge, P. (1990). *The fifth discipline: The art and practice of the learning organisation*. Doubleday.

Sinek, S. (2009). *Start with why: How great leaders inspire everyone to take action*. Portfolio.

Southworth, G. (2009, July). *School leadership: What we know and what it means for schools, their leaders and policy*. Centre for Strategic Education Seminar Series Paper No. 185.

Tuckman, B. W. (1965). *Developmental sequence in small groups. Psychological Bulletin*, *63*(6), 384–399.

van der Kleij, F., Taylor-Guy, P., & Rogers, C. (2023). *School improvement tool: A summary of the underpinning research*. Australian Council for Educational Research.

Wageman, R., Nunes, D., Burruss, J. A., & Hackman, J. R. (2008). *Leadership teams: What it takes to make them great*. Harvard University Press.

7

EFFECTIVE COMMUNICATION AND DECISION-MAKING: CORE CAPABILITIES FOR LEADING A PRODUCTIVE SCHOOL CULTURE

Culture is created one conversation at a time. What we communicate, how we express our core values and what we choose to act upon indicate the culture that we are standing up for.

Cultures can be constructive or destructive. Many people live much of their lives applying zero-sum frameworks. Zero-sum frameworks have clear 'winners' and clear 'losers'. The 'winners' gain status, prestige, money and resources largely at the expense of the 'losers'. Simply, put this is 'little pie' thinking: there is only so much pie to go around, so if you have a big slice, it means that I necessarily, will have a smaller slice.

Of course this is rarely explicitly stated. Nevertheless, it is so ingrained in so many cultures it becomes almost invisible. It is just simply seen as 'the way things are'.

Zero-sum thinking is used to justify oppression. It fuels hierarchies, resentment, envy, protection rackets and social rankings (Sapolsky, 2017). It is often linked with meritocracy where some people are valued in the culture and then attribute their success to some rare traits that they possess that are deficient in others (a.k.a. the 'losers'). Inheritance, circumstances, privilege or just damn good luck are disregarded as potential causes of the 'winner's' success in an attempt to claim exemplary individualism (Sandel, 2021).

Inevitably, zero-sum or *little pie* thinking fuels anxiety. Whatever conditions are seen as desirable, are scarce and need to be fought for. Once acquired, those scarce privileges need to be fiercely guarded from others who would snatch them away, if they only could. Once you have achieved the prizes of life you need high walls and a good security system to prevent those privileges being taken from you.

In contrast, positive-sum thinking is the framework of abundance but is much less popular in a dog-eats-dog kind of world. Simply put, this is 'big pie' thinking: there is plenty of pie to go around and if you have a big slice that's great because if we collaborate, we can create an even bigger pie. Possibilities abound and when we collaborate as a collective community, the sum is always greater than the individual parts. Together we are stronger and smarter than we are alone. None of us is as smart as all of us.

Of course, little pie thinkers regard positive-sum framework thinkers as naïve dupes and as completely bonkers. Constructive leaders are positive-sum, big pie thinkers. And the way they convey that framework is through communication around opportunity and abundance.

Communication is the thread that creates and weaves the culture of any organization. Culture matters, we carry it with us wherever we go.

Leaders have essentially two main types of communication – leading and repairing. Leading involves communication around vision, values and aims to provide a coherent message that gives all members of a school a session of connectedness, coherence and purpose. Repairing involves smoothing out and reorienting people in the community after differences and difficulties (often reflecting *little pie* thinking). Essentially this is the language of healing.

CONNECT

There is a Zulu saying that people are people because of other people. What connects us to others is conversation and the meanings we weave collectively with one another.

In *little pie* cultures, connections between people often descend into social classes, cliques, tribes or gangs. Membership of these groups is as much defined by who the adversaries or enemies of each group as much as what the members share in common. Membership of these gangs must be earned and there are ritualized forms of behaviour to prove the worthiness of each member. This is true whether it be an exclusive club for businesspeople, the Hell's Angels or any number of extremist groups.

Sustaining membership can be a precarious business with indiscretions resulting in exclusion from the group and being cancelled.

Bullying is a disconnection of relationships. Bullies fail to see (or purposely ignore) the humanity in their victims. Almost half of bullying in school is displaced aggression – a stressed student takes it out on other students in an effort to lessen their own stress.

In a connected, protected and respected (CPR) culture connectedness is created through who we are rather than who our adversaries are. It promotes equal membership for all and outlines shared aspirations for the community and values.

Leadership of a CPR culture is a powerful differentiator. We can consider two broad groupings of leaders:

1. Ladder climbers
2. Tapestry weavers.

Ladder climbers create a culture where there are limited places at the top. Opportunities are scarce and advantages are given to those rarest of individuals who are 'worthy' of the positions. Often, there is only one person who can occupy the top rung of the ladder. There is only the tiniest fragment of a slice of the pie to go around right at the top (Gilligan, 2016).

The risk for this type of leader is that while they sit atop the ladder admiring their own worthiness as well as the grand view, they also become disconnected from the worker bees who are busily creating mayhem further down the ladder. Many a fine insurrection has begun in this manner (see J. Ceasar and Brutus for a start!).

Alternatively, tapestry weavers build and strengthen the weave of their culture. There is strong interconnectedness and multiple opportunities to shine. At times there may be some discontent over whether information is shared equitably across the tapestry and over who sits at the centre of the threads, but generally speaking, it is a strong, more enduring and sustainable culture. Nelson Mandela once described this as a 'flamingo culture' – we all take off together.

Communicating for Connection

Given the central space that conversations have in creating a meaningful and happy life, it seems that all of us should set ourselves the goal of becoming better conversationalists.

PROTECT

Creating cultures where people feel safe is essential for learning and wellbeing. However, creating true safety is not always a simple process.

To really get to grips on the intricacies between feeling protected and safe and communication we need to firstly delve into the murky world of honour cultures (Brown, 2016). These are the cultures promoted by misogynists like Andrew Tate and others that threaten the sense of safety for all in our community.

While this certainly doesn't apply to every school or community, it is wise for every school leader to be aware of, and to plan to counter it.

Richard Nisbett's research on honour cultures, particularly in *Culture of Honor: The Psychology of Violence in the South*, highlights how deeply ingrained cultural values shape interpersonal interactions, conflict resolution and social expectations.

At the centre of honour cultures is retribution (Nisbett, 2018). Any perceived sleight or dishonour can justify extreme responses. If someone disrespects you, you feel compelled to retaliate at a heightened level to restore your sense of honour. A failure to respond strongly would be seen as weak, so cycles of retribution usually escalate over time. This can create long-standing feuds and vendettas in which aggression, violence and extremist positions are normalized and intensified. Any person in an honour culture risks becoming a victim if they do not retaliate. This is *little pie* thinking on violent steroids.

Honour cultures often promote traditionalist views of masculinity and militaristic power where displays of strength, toughness and dominance over others are seen as ways young men can prove themselves.

People who tend to adopt honour cultures have a number of common features:

- Families that originated as pastoralists, where if someone stole one of your herd, retaliation was seen as essential to deter further theft.
- Lower economic opportunities for advancement or greater income disparity.
- From countries where institutional authorities such government or the police are seen as unreliable, unstable, self-interested or corrupt.
- New arrivals who feel culturally alienated – they don't feel accepted by their new country and feel they are viewed as betrayers of their ancestral culture (Brown, 2016; Nisbett, 2018; Sapolsky, 2017).

Some honour cultures review their history as a legacy of collective dishonour and consolidate around ideas of making a country great again or redressing the insults inflected upon our people.

Violence is often seen as the only acceptable way to redress these 'insults'. There is an intersection between traditional religious values, honour fuelled retaliation and tribal or gang vendettas. Violence can give young men a sense of purpose and belonging.

In contrast, a **CPR** culture is one that keeps everyone safe though strengthening relationships and collective values. While an honour culture celebrates displays of prowess and strength and the ability to incite fear in, and control others, a **CPR** culture builds respect, conflict resolution and social belonging.

Communicating for Safety

Every leader will be challenged by little pie thinkers who feel that you and your school are ill-preparing their child for the competitive hardships of the 'real' world. One possible way of discussing this is:

> *I understand the concern that focusing on collaboration and compassion might seem naïve in a competitive world. But the real world isn't just about individual survival – it's about alliances, adaptability, and knowing when to compete and when to cooperate. The most successful people,*

leaders, and organisations thrive not by being isolated warriors but by building strong networks, understanding others, and mastering emotional intelligence.

In reality, those who only rely on dominance and self-interest often hit limits – they burn bridges, face resistance, and struggle to lead effectively. The strongest societies and individuals are those who know how to balance personal strength with collective success.

So, teaching young people to be emotionally intelligent, cooperative, adaptable, and strategic in their relationships isn't naïve – it's preparing them to navigate the world with greater influence and long-term success.

Honour cultures thrive on grievance (Brown, 2016). Being humiliated deepens the belief that direct confrontations, displays of strength and the capacity to control and dominate others is justified. For this reason, communication in communities with these cultures needs to be nuanced.

Instead of 'Real men don't fight'.

Try, 'Real strength is protecting others, not proving dominance'.

Instead of, 'Violence makes things worse'.

Try, 'The strongest people are those who build, not destroy'.

Instead of requiring direct apologies

Try, 'I respect you and I don't want conflict between us' (framing peace as strength)

Or, 'We are both bigger than this, let's solve it like leaders'.

Instead of, 'Think for yourself, be your own person' (as in you don't need to follow others)

Try, 'Our community is stronger when we take care of one another'.

Or, 'We rise together by not fighting one another'.

The main themes that are effective with people from honour cultures are:

How can we make things right without creating more harm.
Control is power – letting anger control you is unwise.
Talking about wise warriors.

RESPECT

> *Treat people as if they were what they ought to be, and you help them to become what they are capable of being. (Johann Wolfgang von Goethe)*

As we have seen, honour cultures are run in a negative sense by disrespect. If you disrespect me, I feel compelled to defend myself. Otherwise, I look weak and am vulnerable to future attacks. These are cultures of retribution and tit-for-tat revenge.

In contrast, CPR cultures are determined by collective values and individual agency.

The advantages of a CPR culture include harmony and relationships, being able to consider other peoples' perspectives and the probability of a longer life.

We are more likely to adopt a behaviour if we see three other people doing it which is why leadership in a CPR culture is about modelling respectful behaviours to all.

Essentially a CPR culture is a culture of respectful co-operation.

How Cooperation 'Breaks' Out

Some historians relate human history as a type of unrelenting, violent competition. Thomas Hobbes described life as 'short, brutish and nasty'. Without wanting to whitewash the troubles of history, there are also examples when co-operation and civilization have overridden aggressive impulses.

When people are supported to do so, they prefer peace to war and co-operation to forceful violence. Rather than going into the litany of examples across history, let's briefly touch on two.

The Christmas Truce of 1914 (World War I)

The football matches played in the no-man's land by two warring enemies, German and British soldiers on Christmas Eve 1914 is well known. What is less well known is that peace kept breaking out over subsequent months with soldiers preferring to affiliate and socialize with the enemy rather than to want to kill them (Sapolsky, 2017). It was only under threat of severe consequences that the soldiers reluctantly returned to the business of war.

Environmentalism and Bushfire Responses

Between 1978 and 1983 an unexpected collaboration occurred among environmentalists, Indigenous activists, local residents, and national political parties in Australia to protect with wilderness areas in Tasmania from being dammed. The Franklin River campaign led to a successful outcome, with the High Court ruling to protect and preserve the river.

At numerous times of flooding, bushfires and pandemics, people have collaborated to save other people, often heroically.

How to Build a CPR Culture of Co-operation

If we review the research on co-operation between people, we can see a number of preconditions that increase the likelihood of this occurring.

- People help others with the expectation of being helped in return in the future. It's often.
- Empathy and kindness – a person's capacity to understand and share the feelings of others – is closely tied to cooperative behaviour.
- Oxytocin, Vasopressin and the Biology of Trust – these bonding hormones have been shown to increase trust and cooperation among individuals.
- Having individual requests to help.
- Having rituals that treat newcomers as guests and help them to feel CPR.

- Reinforcing people who have reputations for being co-operative.
- Seeing people as individuals reduces us and them thinking and the sense that there is an in-group and an out-group.
- Shifting people from being bystanders to being upstanders who will speak out when injustices occur. We are more likely to copy a behaviour, if we see three different people do it rather than just one (Sapolsky, 2017).

Communicating for Respect

This is the language that can create possibilities for the people in your community.

This reshapes your role as a possibility creator – what are people's concerns, what skills and resources do I have that are relevant and what future actions are possible. This shifts communication towards the future.

'Here everyone gets smart (in their own way)' is a motto that sets a school on a course for discovering what is great about each person.

Conversations can then focus on:

What skills do you have that we are yet to discover?
What skills would you like to enhance?

A CPR culture, safety is determined by treating people the way you would like to be treated (the golden rule) and strengthen through deep relationships. I'm not going to let you that to someone else because I wouldn't let someone else do that to you.

HIGH-IMPACT COMMUNICATION AND CONVERSATIONS

A single conversation can change a life. Perhaps you can think of time when a comment so touched you, it echoed in your mind until it found a place in your heart. Perhaps there were words of comfort, of support or of understanding that you heard as a child that serve as a cloak against the chill winds of hurt that face us all from time to time.

Great conversations are like enchanting songs sung between people. Conversations harmonize and resonate and deepen our relationships.

The Art of Conversation

Given the central space that conversations have in creating a meaningful and happy life, it seems that all of us should set ourselves of the goal of becoming better conversationalists.

If you can think of some of the wonderful conversations, you have had it is probable that they had some of these features:

People stopped what they were doing and really listened.
Curiosity was piqued.
Jealousy and competition were absent.
Differences were seen as interesting rather than threatening.
People felt able to be authentic and to show their vulnerabilities.
Hurts might have been talked about, but faults were not.
Ideas and humour were played with.

The fine art of talking, getting your message heard and understood as well as converted into some form of action by another human being is an amazingly tricky business.

We all have ongoing conversations with ourselves as well as with others. We can get into all sorts of bother when we project the conversations, we have with ourselves and assume they are the thoughts of others.

It is important to know that:

What is received is not necessarily, what is sent.
What is sent is not always what is meant (Erickson & Rossi, 2022).

The number one most powerful tool to creating impactful conversations with young people is:

Drop everything to be available to talk to.
Be authentic and open your ears.

The Fine Art of Conversational 'Fly Fishing'

Creating high-impact conversations with students is a lot like fly fishing in a stream filled with capricious fish. There are some key skills (Erickson & Rossi, 2022), we can use to become more positively impactful communicators.

Pacing

Pacing involves tuning yourself to someone else's tempo. It can involve breathing at the same rate that they do or matching them where they currently are. Having matched their current behaviour, posture, emotions, language, body signals, you are in a powerful position to understand the way they see the world.

Leading

Having matched the person where they are, you are then in a position to lead them where you want them to go (leading).

At the heart of influential language is presupposition. Presuppositions are the unsaid meanings and information in a sentence or phrases. For example, if someone were to say: 'Either now or in a moment you can think of a time when a conversation has been important to you'. You are very likely to follow this instruction. This is because the first part of the sentence presupposes that you are going to do what has been suggested.

Along with presupposition is linking unrelated events. For example, as you go to the bathroom, I wonder if you could think creatively about this, or, as you spread butter on your toast tomorrow morning I wonder if you will think about what we've said.

Another example of presupposition:

> *You're a genius even though you've forgotten it, just like you've forgotten how you learned to walk.*

Another very useful language technique is the yes set. In this method you make a serious of statements that are undeniably true and then connect them to a suggestion.

For example,

This morning when you got up (Pause, true).
And you still felt sleepy (Pause, true).
And the temptation must have been so strong to stay in bed (Pause, true).
You must have summoned great will power to get to school (Suggestion – yes).

Another example:

Whether you can remember when you were a little kid, there was a time when you were so excited to learn something new.
It might have been dinosaurs, or insects or horses or something even more exciting.
And even though things were confusing, maybe you couldn't even wait to tell someone of your new discovery.
And then one time you learned that it wasn't cool to be quite so excited.
And you learned to cover it up.
You learned to cover it up so well, that now you've almost forgotten where you left it.
Sometimes we hide treasures so well that we don't even realize it.

Seeding

To return to our fly-fishing analogy, pacing is knowing where the fish are, leading them is entrancing them with the possibility of some bait, seeding is knowing which bait to select.

Seeding ideas often takes the form of embedded suggestions and can also be used conversationally.

What do you think people will notice first when you start to free yourself from (the problem)?

As you sleep soundly tonight you may find that clarity emerges in your mind about the direction you want to take, and you can relax into that certainty.

When you start to stop worrying about the things you can't do anything about, I wonder if you'll stop to start focusing on the things you can do to have a happier life.

Seeding and Pacifying Behaviours

We all use pacifying behaviours when we are talking about stressful feelings. Teens are masters at this. They twist their hair, look at their feet, touch their face, scratch, yawn, roll their eyes, exhale more loudly than usual, fiddle with things or shake their legs. Notice how people self-soothe and pacify their feelings.

An increase in pacifying actions is often an indication that someone is becoming more agitated or even potentially aggressive. Lower the tone of the interaction at this point.

A stillness of pacifying actions often indicates a moment when new ideas or associations can be seeded into the conversation.

While you can incorporate all of these methods to increase the impact of conversations with young people, it is essential to remain authentic. Words make a powerful difference and especially when they are spoken by a kind person who genuinely has your best interests at heart.

The Language of Empowerment

We also want to shift people away from words that lessen their power to change their situation. Often young people talk in ways that frame themselves as a hapless victim of unfortunate circumstances. The words they use to convey this sense are useful to notice because eventually you may wish to shift them to using words that are more powerful.

Building Constructive Conversations

Don't stay around to be abused. Some people are yet to learn that demeaning, abusing language doesn't work. It is ok to say to them, 'I don't have to put up with being spoken to like that. When you are ready to talk positively, I'll be happy to chat with you'. Then move away.

From	Replace with
I have to	I choose to
I need	I want
I can't	I won't
I'm afraid to	I'd like to
Maybe/try	Will or won't
I can't stand	I don't like
Hopeless	Stuck
Other methods	

In a family setting it is ok to say, 'we don't speak to one another in that way' and then move away.

Stay Cool and Collected

Some people love drama and intensify interactions. Take your sails out of their winds. If you become aware that you are feeling threatened or agitated, pause, find some other task that you need to do and settle yourself.

Practice Flying Reminders

If someone is speaking disrespectfully, quietly whisper to them, 'you're better than this, drop it' and move on.

CONVERSATIONS TO HAVE WITH YOUR SCHOOL

If your school could talk, what do you think it would say to you?
Where would it feel it was functioning with intentionality and clarity of purpose?
Where would it feel bogged down?
Where would it feel like to require great effort to achieve positive outcomes?
What would be its frustrations? What would it be pleased with?
Where would it think you are making a difference?
Where would it say you are squandering your energies?

CONVERSATIONS TO HAVE WITH YOURSELF

The most powerful conversation of all is the one you have with yourself. Try to allocate one hour a week to sit down with in a quiet place with a private notebook with the intention of uncovering and resolving the internal conversation you are having around an important question. Develop a question worthy of a one-hour noble conversation and then sit with your thoughts, noting ideas as you go. There will be times in the hour when your ideas dry up. Persist. Sit there for the entire hour. Our best thoughts are late arrivers. This could well be the most important conversation you have each week.

DECISION-MAKING

It is almost impossible for school leaders to make a bad decisions if they place the interests of their students at the heart of every decision they make. This simplifies the competing demands and priorities confronting the decision-making process.

Harvesting and Hunting

In any school or community there are un-actualized strengths and treasures.

Capitalizing on those unpacked treasures is the process of harvesting. These are the 'scale-ups' in your school or community. Discovering the submerged or neglected strengths and amplifying them, not only recognizes the contribution of community members it also shifts the focus of the school towards strengths. These are the foundations of decision-making that may not always be immediately apparent.

Additionally, there are possibilities that need to be sought out or 'hunted'. These are the 'start-ups' of your school or community – the activities that are not yet happening that you would like to see. Schools can only embrace so much change and development at a time.

Deciding how much time is allocated to harvesting and hunting will depend on the current circumstances.

Decision-making for school leaders is always a complex series of trade-offs. Every decision has implications in terms of human power, time and money.

Changes in priorities are always accompanied by changes in the allocation of resources.

It is always worth asking yourself:

1. What is the upside?

This is not always a clear as it sounds, the upside compared to what. Every decision we make has an opportunity cost. By opting for one position, we neglect another (Cunningham, 2017).

While it would be nice to say, use data to inform your decision-making, often you won't have complete data. Not everything that counts can be counted and not everything that counted counts.

Questions worth considering are:

Compared with what?
And then what?
At the expense of what?

2. What is the downside?

Similarly, downsides are not always clear or foreseeable. Outlining different scenarios can be helpful.

3. Can I live with the downside?

In the world of trade-offs caution is advisable. When in doubt, stall for time and analyse and consider deeply (Cunningham, 2017).

Triadic Decision-making

Attempting to succeed by trial and error is stupid, slow and expensive. It helps no one to spend longer than necessary practising the wrong things. If we want to do better, we need to get better and that requires careful planning and decision-making (Cunningham, 2017).

Human brains want to simplify most complex issues down to a choice between two options – that or that, now or then, here or there, yes or no (Sapolsky, 2017). Life is rarely so straightforward for leaders.

When we shift from either/or decision-making and include a third option, we increase the quality and depth of our consideration and decision.

PICCA

To help us remember how to do this it's useful to employ an acronym called PICCA (Fuller, 2024a, 2024b), which stands for a five-step way of making decisions:

1. Problem
2. I want
3. Choices
4. Compare
5. Act.

Problem

The first thing to do is to clarify what the problem or decision you need to make is. Generally, the need for a decision arises when there is a problem. What's the issue?

At first glance, stating what the problem is may seem very straightforward, but it is also important to get it right.

For example, a review of the railroad system in 1975 concluded:

> *The railroads did not stop growing because the need for passenger and freight transportation declined. That grew. The railroads are in trouble today not because the need was filled by others (cars, trucks, airplanes, even telephones), but because it was not filled by the railroads themselves. They let others take customers away from them because they assumed themselves to be in the railroad business rather than in the transportation business.*

Try out a few different ways of expressing the problem. One of the ways to clarify what the problem is, is to ask yourself five 'why' questions. For example:

I feel that we need to refresh our offerings to our community. *Why?*

Enrolments are slightly lower this year *Why?*

A new school has opened in the area. *Why?*
Population has increased, but enrolments here have not *Why? Why?*

I Want

These are also known as objectives but really, they are the things, that matter, the things that you want. Very few people specify what they want. Or they specify it in such a wishy-washy way that even they are unsure whether they have achieved it.

When we clarify what we want, we put our power of intentionality to work.

One way to do this is to shift from asking people what they want to do to making invitations and proposals. For example, rather than saying to a friend or partner, 'Let's catch up. What would you like to do?' say, 'There's a movie on at the cinema I'd like to see. Would you like to come with me?'

Let's build a PICCA decision matrix (see Table 7) using an example of a leader who wants to consider developing a new programme for school and the physical resources that might be involved.

Problem or issue – *How to best accommodate 100 additional students in Year 8.*

Choices

Now consider three main ways that this could be achieved, as shown in Table 8.

Compare

Difficult decisions usually have a trade-off, and it's usually not a straightforward matter. For this reason, it's worth drawing up a comparison table, as shown in Table 9, using a five-star rating scale.

Action

Which matters more – if I absolutely had to choose between these options which matters more.

What are your success criteria?

Post it notes one for each criterion.

Table 7. PICCA – Outlining the Desired Outcomes.

I want
Students to feel safe and excited about learning
Parents to be excited about the prospects of the new programme
To provide a cutting edge research-based programme
To have staff who are excited to work in the programme
Keep costs low or at least use them on the programme

Table 8. PICCA – Triadic Ways to Ach.ieve Desired Outcomes.

	Construct a New Building	Repurpose an Existing Building	Have Real-world Learning with Minimal Meetup Places and Some Shared Workspaces
I want			
Students to feel safe and excited about learning			
Parents to be excited about the prospects of the new programme			
To provide a cutting-edge research-based programme			
To have staff who are excited to work in the programme			
Keep costs low or at least use them on the programme			

Table 9. PICCA – Comparing the Options to Achieve Desired Outcomes.

	Construct a New Building	Repurpose an Existing Building	Have Real-world Learning with Minimal Meetup Places and Some Shared Workspaces
I want			
Students to feel safe and excited about learning	***	***	*****
Parents to be excited about the prospects of the new programme	*****	****	***
To provide a cutting-edge research-based programme	****	****	*****
To have staff who are excited to work in the programme	***	**	****
Keep costs low or at least use them on programme delivery	*	***	******

Make your criteria battle with one another until you can rank them in importance.

Now apply them to your options.

DEVELOPING THE ART OF DECISION-MAKING

Obviously, there are much more complex decision-making models you can access but I find PICCA to be sufficient for most children and fairly easy to work through with them.

Of course, once you have decided about the direction you want to go in, it's then a matter of being motivated to start it and stick with it.

KEY IDEAS

- Communication is at the very heart of building a CPR culture.
- A CPR culture can be contrasted with an honour culture.
- This chapter outlines a rationale and process for creating this.

REFERENCES

Brown, R. P. (2016). *Honor bound – How a cultural idea has shaped the American psyche*. Oxford University Press.

Cunningham, K. J. (2017). *The road less stupid, keys to the vault.* Greenleaf Book Group Press.

Erickson, M. H., & Rossi, E. (2022). *The collected works of Milton H. Erickson, Volume 3 – Opening the mind*. Roxanna Erickson-Klein.

Fuller, A. (2024a). *Tricky conversations – How to have less conflict and more peace in your life*. Amba Press.

Fuller, A. (2024b). *Unlocking your child's genius – How to build your child's learning strengths*. Amba Press.

Gilligan, C. (2016). *In a different voice: Psychological theory and women's development.* Harvard University Press.

Nisbett, R. E. (2018). *Culture of honor: The psychology of violence in the south*. Routledge.

Sandel, M. J. (2021). *The Tyranny of Merit: What's become of the common good?* Penguin.

Sapolsky, R. M. (2017). *Behave – The biology of humans at our best and worst*. Penguin Random House UK.

8

PERSUADING AND INFLUENCING, THE CULTURAL CHANGE NARRATIVE – THE POWER OF STORYTELLING

> *Stories are the single most powerful weapon in a leader's arsenal. (Howard Gardiner, 1995)*

Leadership by its very nature involves persuading and influencing others to do things, implementing a new curriculum, contributing to the strategic direction of the school, supporting others and complying with legislation, to name but a few. How do school leaders engage, support and inspire the various stakeholders in a school setting? How do they persuade and influence ideas and enact agreed decisions that will contribute to building cultural collateral? Building culture as previously noted is an ongoing and incomplete behaviour and disposition of any school leader. A critical capability for any leader to sustain and constantly animate what the desired and aspired culture for any school is through storytelling:

> *Leaders are storytellers. All great organisations are born from a compelling story. This central organising thought helps people understand what they stand for a why. (Kerr, 2013, p. 144)*

Knowing that stories are an essential and valued component of organizational culture, school leaders can re-set and redefine the culture of any school by curating and telling stories about key aspects of the organization such as students, data, staff achievements and community feedback. Stories play a vital role in contributing to school culture because they help shape its identity, values and a sense of connection, belonging and community. Narratives about students, teachers, school leaders and alumnus who demonstrate a school's values make those values real. Stories provide the stimulus for people to feel a sense of belonging when they reflect their own aspirations, experiences and their voice acknowledged.

Another important thing about stories is that they tell how the rituals, events, traditions and history that form the school's culture are preserved. Leaders who use stories effectively and strategically can build a deeper relationship by sharing a little of who they are, what they stand for and what they value. It follows that by being vulnerable and declarative about their professional identity, the enhancement of professional relationships results. In times of transition and change, leaders can use stories to explain the why behind decisions and approaches adopted to an initiative. They are also sense makers in terms of uncertainty using stories in times of disruption to interpret the circumstances of the moment and to provide hope for others they lead. Bennis (1996) argues that storytelling is a central leadership skill because stories give meaning, create identity and inspire action. Leaders are not just in the business of manufacturing decisions, they are narrative creators who help people understand who they are, where they are going and why it matters.

> *The most powerful person in the world is the storyteller. The storyteller sets the vision, values and agenda of an entire generation that is to come. (Steve Jobs)*

Neuro-economist Paul Zak (2014) has found that hearing a story, a narrative with a beginning, middle and end causes our brains to release cortisol and oxytocin. These trigger the uniquely human ability to control, empathize and make meaning. We are literally storytelling and being open to persuasion and influence is literally in our DNA:

> *What is distinctively human is at the most fundamental level the capacity to persuade and be persuaded. (Bertrand Russell, 1927)*

We are literally hard wired as humans to tell stories as a core means of transferring knowledge, keeping cultural habits, rituals alive, and communication in general. Fletcher (2023) notes that 'story thinking' existed from the earliest history of humanity and is our first technology as people.

How do school leaders' harness and master the power of storytelling to persuade and influence others? What are the approaches and techniques that can be adopted to enable increased proficiency in this key aspect of leadership practice?

Aristotle's, *On Rhetoric* contends that effective persuasion depends on establishing a sturdy tripod of three components: *logos, pathos and ethos. Logos* are the rational, logical aspects of any person's argument. Such aspects are typified and represented using statistics, key points, data, facts and analogies. *Ethos* is essentially about a leader or speaker's individual and professional credibility. In short, is the leader likeable, able to evoke a sense of trustworthiness and is acknowledged as having subject expertise and can demonstrate a connection with the group, stakeholders and/or target audience. *Pathos* refers to the ability of a speaker and a leader to engage with the audience and their emotions, motivating people to take an interest in issues that require a collective focus and commitment. Orren (2001) proposes two additional 'legs' for leaders to consider in making an impact on others – agora and syzygy. *Agora* is about where and when. Specifically, where is about considering such things as the venue, setting, culture and resources. *Syzygy* is from the Greek *syn*, to join, and *sygon*, to yoke. In nature, this is the rare alignment of celestial bodies, such as the sun, moon and the earth during an eclipse, influencing the earth's gravitational system. In terms of persuasion, it is about aligning, combining and balancing ethos, pathos, logos and agora. Leaders, when considering how to persuade and influence others should consider the *LEAPS* (*Logos, Ethos, Agora, Pathos and Syzygy*) elements to frame their approach. Gardiner (1995) in his work, *Leading Minds: An Anatomy of Leadership* notes that there are the following six key constants of leadership (Gardiner, 1995):

1. *Story*: A leader must have a central story or message.
2. *Audience:* The audience must be ready to hear the story.

3. *Organization*: Enduring leadership ultimately demands some institutional or organizational basis.
4. *Embodiment*: The creator must in some sense embody her/his story, so as not to appear hypocritical.
5. *Direct/indirect leadership*: The transition is easier from indirect leadership (domain specific) to direct leadership (more heterogenous).
6. *Issue of expertise*: Within a domain, an individual is unlikely to achieve credibility unless her/his work is seen to be of high quality. Within every domain, there is technical knowledge unavailable to most leaders or audience members. The leader must be able to call on that knowledge when needed.

To influence a person/group's behaviour or attitude any message or narrative must appeal or motivate a target audience. Robert Cialdini (1984) in his text, *Influence: The Psychology of Persuasion* identified seven principles of influence shown in Table 10: reciprocity, commitment and consistency, social proof, authority, liking, scarcity and unity.

Orren (2001) suggests that there are four predominant approaches to social influence. These are:

1. Power, the use by leaders of a command/control style, assertiveness, force, coercion, threat and intimidation.
2. Payment, such an approach is typified by inducements such as material incentives, rewards, compensation and, at the extreme, bribery.
3. Negotiation, such an approach is characterized by bargaining, exchange between individuals or parties to an issue, trading with the overall intention to arrive at a joint decision.
4. Persuasion, which is ultimately for any leader effectively communicating in a way that induces others to voluntarily think or act differently.

School leaders can consciously craft stories and hone their individual capability in this aspect to their leadership practices that foster productive school cultures. Stories are a much underutilized leadership capability to communicate and enable the translation of

Table 10. Cialdini's 7 Principles of Influence (1984).

Reciprocity	People feel obligated to give back to others when they have received something first. For example, if someone gives another person a free sample of something, then the recipient is more predisposed to giving the person time to deliver their message.
Commitment and consistency	People want to be consistent with what they have previously said or done. For example, many retailers use written commitments to match prices of other competitors. In school, staff consistently act in accordance with stated policies.
Social Proof	The essence of this principle is that people will look at the behaviour of others to determine their own. This is important to consider when endeavouring the intercede into aspects of a school's culture and current climate.
Authority	People are more likely to be influenced by individuals they perceive as credible experts or authority figures. This principle is aligned with Aristotle's, recognition of ethos as a key characteristic in influencing others to engage with ideas, arguments and a change agenda.
Liking	Individuals are more easily persuaded by people they connect with and they like. This is another reminder of the crucial importance of quality relationship being at the heart of thriving school culture. Relationships in which people feel connected, protected and respected. Leaders who genuinely fostered connection in their school have a necessary pre-condition to influence others for the common good and a shared aspiration.
Scarcity	Things become more desirable when they are perceived as rare or limited in availability. For example, many schools use the lure of limited places in certain grades or phases as a tactic to attract enrolments.
Unity	People are more influenced by those they share an identity with, such as family, classmates, sporting team players, suburb or family background. Again, this signals the importance of building a school culture that stakeholders can identify and connect with. As described previously, within any school there will be microcultures that exist within the school's overall cultural and climate dynamic.

a school's strategic intentions. Each leader will have a preferred or default style and approach to communicating and delivering their message. Bowden (2022) contends that there are four typical persuasive personality types that use different predominant emphases to convince and influence others. These types using a bird-type analogy are the metaphorical wise owl; tending to establish their credibility through their message; the commanding eagle; persuading through personal authority; the friendly budgie; who focuses on building goodwill with others around them and the captivating peacock; who attempts to derive influence by arousing enthusiasm and passion. Dolan and Naidu's (2015) story intelligence model suggest that there are four distinct types of business storytellers: (1) the avoider – low engagement and low purpose; (2) the joker – high engagement and low purpose; (3) the reporter – low engagement and high purpose; and (4) the inspirer – high engagement and high purpose. They suggest that such styles are determined by two criteria: how engaging the story is and whether the person's story has a strong purpose. Such a matrix provides another way for a school leader to reflect on their areas for further growth in developing their story telling capabilities shifting and aspiring to high engagement and high purpose.

Cultural change should be story powered. Such stories cannot be solely constructed on perceived facts, figures, numbers and case studies. A dependence on logos won't convince the people leaders are trying to influence. Data needs a story, and stories need to have data (Orren, 2002). Research indicates that decision-making is predominantly informed and driven 90% of the time by a person's emotions (Comaford, 2013; Dolan & Naidu, 2015).

There is no one formula that leaders can adopt to create that compelling narrative that will persuade and influence to voluntarily change behaviours and practices. In its crudest and rudimentary form, any story should have a key message, a start, a middle and a conclusion, an ending. Abraham Lincoln's 272 word, Gettysburg Address amplifies that less is more in terms of storytelling. Ultimately, it is a leadership judgement about length.

From the literature there are a range of storytelling frameworks and associated techniques that school leaders could consider in refining and deeping their story telling capabilities.

The Leadership Narrative Arc approach has the following distinct but interrelated components: (a) *the origin or founding story* – where did the school's writing programme commence or when did the school introduce a certain approach to pastoral care of students or when was the school established and why?; (b) what are some of the key events or *defining moments* that have shaped the programmes and or the direction of the school; (c) what the next stage, *the aspiration(s) for the future* and why?; and (d) the all important call to action. *The Leadership Narrative Arch* has direct applicability to school activities such as staff induction and strategic planning.

The classic model of *Joseph Campbell's, Hero's Journey* provides another useful approach for school leaders to develop narratives that inspire and connect. The phases of this approach are: (a) the establishment of a start point or commentary on the status quo – *the ordinary world*; (b) *the call to adventure* – a challenge or opportunity emerges for a school and its community for example; (c) *struggle and growth* – obstacles are faced, challenged, resolved and overcome; (d) *transformation* – this is the reflective commentary typified by language such as lessons learnt and example of change acknowledged; and (e) return – the 'hero' or leader(s) bring enhanced wisdom and success to the school community. Such a technique has applicability and resonance in helping a leader describe their personal leadership journey and could be used to tell a narrative about whole school change.

The *Five Cs* storytelling approach commences with the leader (1) setting the scene – the *context*; (2) who was or is involved, *the characters*; (3) *conflict*, what challenge(s) are to be or were faced; (4) what was the *climax* or turning point?; and (5) the conclusion, lessons learnt and what has been achieved.

The above is a sample of the various approaches that leaders could consider in crafting what should and must be a uniquely personal style suitable to the uniqueness of each leader and the setting in which they are undertaking their work. Previous chapters have explored other models such as Sinek and the adaptive approach that school leaders could use to develop their storytelling fluency.

However, there are common criteria commentated on above that school leaders should reflect upon in shaping a narrative designed to enable change (Dolan, 2017; Kerr, 2013):

- The story must be credible and relevant in Aristotelian terms; it must have ethos (an authority and understanding of the subject matter) and logos (it must make rational sense).
- It must be visual and visceral appealing to the auditory, visual and kinaesthetic aspects of people's brains. In Aristotelian poetics, it must have pathos (it must be felt).
- It must be flexible and scalable – expressed and conveyed in everyday language.
- It must be useful conveying a connection to the school's purposes and practices.
- It must be real, believable, authentic and have a clear intended purpose.

In shaping any change story, school leaders should consider what they can realistically influence and change. Covey's (1989) three circles of control, influence and concern provide a point of reflection for a leader when considering where to focus the energy of a school: (a) circle of concern – this represents the broader range of concerns that an individual have little or no direct control over such as school funding and government policy changes in relation to school curriculum; (b) circle of influence – are the things that a person, a school leader can influence but don't have total control over such as communication and staff relationships; and (c) a person's or leaders circle of control are the things that they have direct control over such as their action, responses and language.

WINNING HEARTS AND MINDS

The perennial challenge for any school leader and leaders in general is to connect with and win the hearts and minds of people.

In any school, like all organizations, there is a communication network. It is a complex set of relationships, systems and mechanisms by which information is transferred, meaning made, stories created, myths born and re-enforced. School leader who consciously consider and map the nature of this network can use such insights to enable cultural change.

A useful taxonomy of the roles that exist with the network are the (a) *story tellers*; (b) *spies*; (c) *priests and priestesses*; (d) *whisperers*; and (e) *cabals*. The story tellers as the name suggests use stories to reinforce the cultural mores of a school. *School spies* are the individuals who pride themselves on knowing what is happening, for other people and around the organization. The *priests and priestesses* are the staff members who are typically well respected by their peers and are guardians of the school values. School leaders would be wise to ensure that are acknowledged and opinions sought when considering and enabling cultural change. *Whisperers* are the individuals on staff who may not have formal positional authority, but they use informal processes to provide feedback and information to decision-makers. The *cabals* are what can be described as a combination of staff members who galvanize for a common purpose.

For any story to be successful, it obviously must connect with the intended audience(s). Culture does indeed eat strategy for breakfast (attributed to Peter Drucker). For any school leader, it is useful to analyse their stakeholders and to reflect upon the messaging of the story they wish to enunciate. The types and factions within typical school stakeholder group can be dissected according to interests, level or degree of power and attitude or predominant mindsets and relationship with the school's leaders. In Table 11, stakeholders can be plotted by power and influence against the group's aspirations and placed into four groups, shown in Fig. 4: keep close; keep satisfied; keep informed and minimal effort.

Another approach is for a leader to reflect upon the current level of influence and mindset that exists with a school community towards an issue, change, attitude towards the school leadership and other dynamic factors, as shown in Fig. 5. This figure provides a strategy for any school leader to plot that stakeholder or audience for the narrative according to level of influence and attitude.

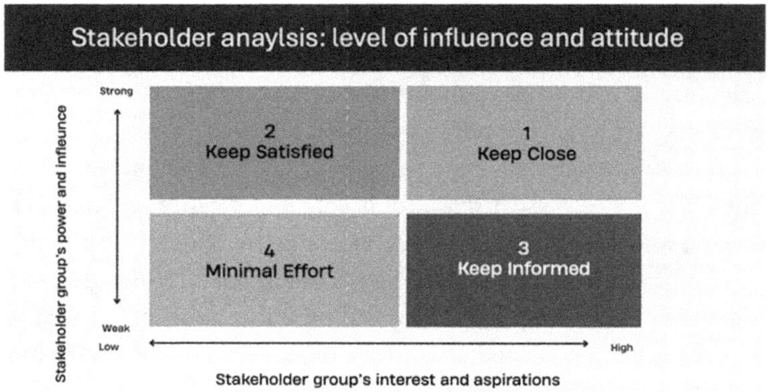

Fig. 4 Stakeholder's Interests and Influence Matrix.

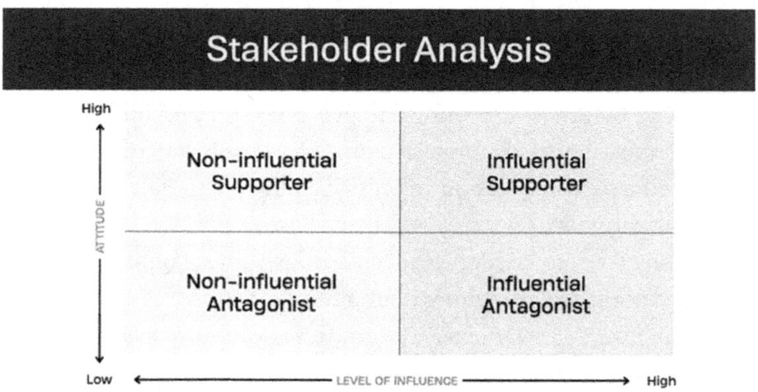

Fig. 5 Stakeholder Analysis: Level of Influence and Attitude.

Gardiner (1995) provides a useful and fascinating perspective about understanding an audience. He states that it is comparable to a contestable four distinct developmental phases of an individual's mind – the five-year-old mind, the ten-year-old one, the adolescent mind and the actualized, mature one (see Table 11). Each of these phases of maturation and sophistication of an individual's mind also means a different, more refined view of change and the world around them. So, what are the applicability for a school leader and storytelling? In short, it confirms what can be observed in organizations like schools that some stakeholders have and don't have a sophisticated approach to engaging with a proponent of a story.

Table 11. The Audience (Gardiner, 1995).

The Five-Year-Old Mind
• Limited ability to empathize with others. • Sees the world in terms of good versus evil. • Belong to one group only: family, church or state.
The Ten-Year-Old Mind
• Fair to a fault. • Consider the intention underlying an action, as well as the action itself. • Spurn those whom they consider bad. • Acknowledge the existence of different groups and try to identify with positive groups.
The Adolescent Mind
• See people as having both good and bad traits. • Friendships are dynamic and changing. • Believe groups have long and complex histories; no one group has a copyright on goodness or evil.
The Mature Mind
• Synthesize warning viewpoints, but take a stand on what they personally believe in. • Concerned with what they have accomplished and how they are regarded in the community. • Will choose a specific group and justify its position but realize that if they were members of another group they might think differently.

FOR REFLECTION AND DISCUSSION

1. Reflect on your storytelling capabilities. How do you use these in your leadership?
2. What aspect(s) of your story telling capabilities are your strength(s) and what aspects could you improve?
3. Think about the context of your school. In your leadership role, what is something that you are passionate about and can influence?
4. Thinking about the staff at your school or schools you have worked with or at. Discuss the application of the types of roles to the communication network that exists.

5. Construct a story about a key initiative, idea, change you need to convey to a key group that you lead. Use one of the storytelling models and the LEAPS framework to guide your preparation.
6. Use the stakeholder mapping matrix entitled, stakeholder matrix to map how different groups and factions within your circle of influence will see the initiative, idea or proposition for change?
7. Reflect on your leadership and others that you work or engage with. Do you embody your story, your credo. Do you 'walk' your talk?

KEY IDEAS

- Storytelling is an essential leadership skill.
- Aristotle's three components of effective persuasion-logos, pathos and ethos.
- The LEAPS approach (Orren, 2001) to persuading and influencing-logos, ethos, agora, pathos and syzygy.
- Gardiner's (1995) Constants of Leadership.
- Cialdini's (1984) Seven Principles of Influence.
- Four predominant approaches to social influence: power, payment, negotiation and persuasion (Orren, 2001).
- Story telling frameworks selective options: The Leadership Narrative Arc; The Hero's Journey and the Five C approach.
- Common criteria for school leaders to consider when creating a change story.
- The communication network within any school and archetypal roles that people play within this aspect of any school's culture-story tellers, spies, priests and priestesses, whisperers and cabals.
- Engaging with stakeholders' framework according to key criteria: influence, attitude, perceived and or actual power.

REFERENCES

Bennis, W. (1996, January–February). The leader as storyteller. *Harvard Business Review*.

Bowden, M. (2022). *How to persuade: The skills you need to get what you want*. John Wiley & Sons.

Cialdini, R. B. (1984). *Influence: How and why people agree to things*. William Morrow & Company.

Comaford, C. (2013). *Smart tribes: How teams become brilliant together*. Penguin Books.

Covey, S. (1989). *The seven habits of highly effective people – Powerful lessons in personal change*. Fireside Books, Simon & Schuster.

Dolan, G. (2017). *Stories for work: The essential guide to business storytelling*. John Wiley & Sons.

Dolan, G., & Naidu, Y. (2015). *Hooked: How leaders connect, engage and inspire with story telling*. John Wiley & Sons.

Fletcher, A. (2023). *Storythinking – The new science of narrative intelligence*. Columbia University Press.

Gardiner, H. (1995). *Leading minds – An anatomy of leadership*. Basic Books.

Kerr, J. (2013). *Legacy: What the All Blacks can teach us about the business of life*. Constable.

Orren, G. (2001). *Persuasion: The science and art of effective influence*. John F. Kennedy School of Government, Harvard University, Australian Institute of Management Master Class course notes.

Orren, G. (2002). *Persuasion: The science and art of effective influence* (Australian Institute of Management Masterclass course notes). Australian Institute of Management.

Russell, B. (1927). *Outline of philosophy*. George Allen & Unwin.

Zak, P. (2014). *Why your brain loves good storytelling*. Harvard Business Review.

9

CULTURE: BUILD ONE CONVERSATION AND ONE INTERACTION AT A TIME

Any leader embarking on the process of culture change in a school is essentially in the business of coaching teams towards success. The process of leading a school culture from where it is currently, to having people feel connected, protected and respected (CPR), takes us from persuasion and influence to coaching your school team for a shift in the way they act.

Even though feeling CPR are basic human psychological needs, people who are not accustomed to having these needs met or have not experienced this level of support will initially experience this as a jolt. As mentioned in the previous chapter, these are either influential or non-influential antagonists.

We use as our coaching model, the well-known *Ready, Set, Go*:

Ready – getting into the right mindset to create the shift, both individually and as a team.

Set – spreading the contagion of change and sustaining it when the first challenge (inevitably) tests the resolve of the team.

Go – amplifying and creating a cascade of positive impacts and preparing for the next time momentum needs to be shifted.

READY

Let's Get Cracking

As obstacles mount up, it is easy to allow what is not working to absorb our focus. We want to be realistic about the challenges we face; we want to prepare our team to create a turn-around. Shirking the challenges and hoping for the best isn't going to cut it. We need to summon strengths and shared purpose.

Remove All Distractions

You don't need a retreat – you need an intensive. During the intensive phase of planning and getting ready, eliminate all distractions. Phones should either be face-down and on silent or even better out of the room. Lap top lids should be down. No interruptions. No extraneous people.

While having a balance of activities is the basis of a good lifestyle and prevents burnout, it is kryptonite for intensive shifts. To shift culture, you need your team to be obsessively focused on creating different outcomes.

It is prolonged consideration and discussions held face to face that will activate your influential supporters and calm and regulate your influence antagonists.

Success Is a Habit, Not a Stroke of Luck

Achieving success is the result of small, deliberate actions taken over time. Schools who are successful don't rely on luck or chance but on the discipline to form and maintain habits that drive them towards their goals. Hard workers get 'lucky'. It is not a one-time event, it's a continuous, incremental process built on repeated positive actions. As Seneca suggested *Luck = Preparation x Opportunity.*

What We Stand For

We connect over shared purpose and the way we relate to one another. We may not be able to control all the external circumstances, but we are in charge of how we act in the future. These shifts don't begin when you start moving – it begins with how you prepare.

Cultural change begins when we deeply look into our own values and integrity and remind ourselves of what we stand for.

Great teams don't make less mistakes than less highly performing teams, but they do recover from them faster.

When setbacks occur, we fix them. We don't finger point, we don't blame or find fault, we don't bicker or squabble, we fix it. We can't always control all the outcomes, but we step up and act in ways that are true to our brand and our values.

The culture of any team is the way people relate to one another. It is the relationships between people that create high performing school cultures, and treating people well, is what we as a group stand for.

Great school teams move everyone forward in contribution and team members develop a sense of loyalty and trust in every member when mistakes are made.

Effective school cultures always give and take from every member, and every member is consistently being acknowledged for their contribution. People are encouraged to take risks.

The most contestable space is between the team members' ears. In challenging circumstances, there is usually at least one team member who thinks that suggested changes don't apply to them. The most stubborn resistance can be from passive inertia and vested interests within the team.

Leadership within the team overrides this. Empower the team to decide to take collective, calculated risks and to support and hold one another accountable for creating shifts.

We might as well act with daring and take lessons from it. Let's aim to play creatively and wildly. Taking risks is energizing and freeing. Don't give up, cut loose.

As Charles Darwin noted, *it is not the strongest species that survive, nor the most intelligent but the most adaptable.*

Peak Performance Mindset

In uncertain moments, leadership creates clarity and unifies purpose. When teams know what's in their control, and what success looks like – confidence rises and wasted effort lessens (see Fig. 6). That's a win in any environment, but it's critical when things feel volatile.

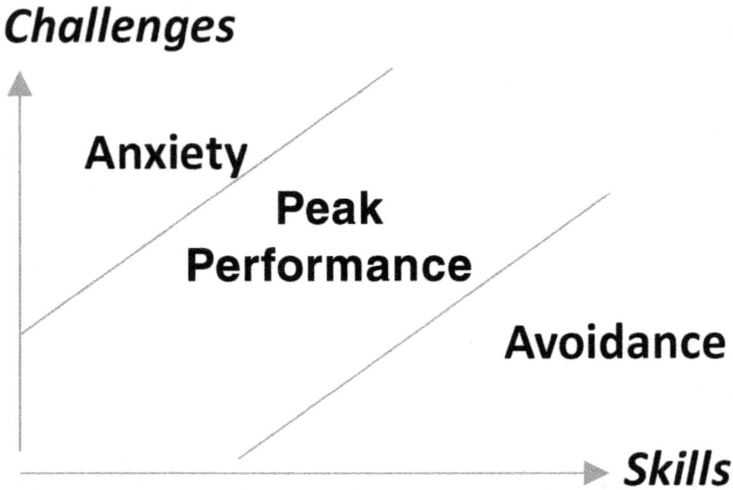

Fig. 6 Peak Performance Challenges.

Different team members will need different types of leadership to regain a high-performance mindset. Some may feel bruised by not having succeeded and need your trust and support. Others may be too eager to rectify the balance sheet, and their anxiety can convert into reckless optimism.

Optimism does not sustainably shift culture. Optimism especially when mixed with stress is the breakfast food of failure. This is not about pep talks or hoping for the best plan to be daring and take our chances while leveraging our strengths.

Successful culture change is a product of *psychological readiness, mental resilience and timely activation*. When teams know how to shift or recover their vision of shared purpose, they become more confident, flexible and resilient.

Accountability isn't just a conversation about standards. It's a leadership decision – to create clarity in uncertainty, positive changes in complex circumstances and performance that lasts.

Focus on Process Not Outcomes

Segment performance into controllable goals. Establish milestones or KPI's for the next month.

Train in High-pressure Situations

There is a reason why we practice in private to perform in public. We want to rehearse changing culture by experiencing pressure during training.

Simulating high-stakes moments in practice, inoculates teams to stress. Ideally, train at a greater intensity than we are likely to need. Anticipate as many things you can that could go wrong and prepare responses. This automates decision-making in high-pressure moments. It creates a culture of creativity rather than reactivity.

Thinking under pressure as a thought-exercise prepares teams for quick decisive action when immediacy is required. Build scenarios for every adversity you can imagine then treat these as challenges, *How would we handle it if.*

Game scenarios with time-constricted decision-making protocols.

Amplify Confidence-based Language

Where possible, pause to imagine success.

Mental imagery activates brain areas similar to physical execution, reducing anxiety.

Cognitive priming helps team members visualize success to activate goal-directed behaviours. Believing in limits creates limited beliefs.

For example, imagining taking a winning shot increases the probability of doing so in basketball.

A business example involves the United Parcel Service who implemented ORION (On-Road Integrated Optimization and Navigation) where drivers visualized delivery routes. The results indicated an increase in efficiency and annual savings of between 300 and 400 million dollars a year.

Expect to Find a Way

Success is always uneven and can never be guaranteed but setbacks don't last forever.

Teams that develop a shared identity of success are less prone to fear of failure.

An example is a team reinforcing *We are a team that starts the year well and finishes the year stronger* helps build a culture of success in tight circumstances.

Anchor and Ritualize Confidence

We don't just connect, we gather. When teams act in synchrony with one another, they perform better pre-performance routines and rituals help trigger a familiar, confident state.

Clarifying plans, role/task clarity in projects, readiness checklists, first steps and first outcomes build this.

A sporting example is a swimmer splashing water on their face before a race to signal readiness.

We're All in This Together – Reinforce Shared Purpose

Shared group identity enhances cohesion and willingness to exert effort. Team rituals, shared language or symbols, and collective planning and goal setting.

When Gary Kirsten coached the Indian Cricket team to winning the World Cup he transformed the team from a group of exceptionally talented individuals to an exceptionally talented team.

Create Pre-performance Rituals

Prepare is the same way for peak performance and momentum shifts. Consistent physical, mental and emotional cues (e.g., warm-up rhythm, team handshake, motto).

The message needs to be, *This is who we are. This is what we're aiming for. The way we do anything is the way we do everything.*

READY CHECKLIST

Ready is when belief is built, trust is renewed, and intention is clarified. Teams that invest in this stage don't just perform better; they bounce back faster when things get messy.

Set okay, you've aligned the purposes of the team, you have soothed and re-oriented those who have felt full of doubt and defeat. You have gently tempered the vigour of those who want to solve any current deficiencies by single-handed heroics. We have even calmed the believers who despite all prevailing recent evidence have faith that a miraculous turn-around will 'just happen'.

We are ready to act.

Set is the moment just before the explosive launch. In workplaces, it's the moment before the big pitch, the tough deadline, or the high-stakes collaboration. This isn't just a pause, it's a mental crucible.

It is often at our moments before taking on major undertakings that doubts nibble away at our confidence. Doubt, fear and memory of past failures all surge at this time. Unconscious self-sabotage behaviours can occur at this time. Carl Jung wrote of this as the shadow part of a team's collective psyche.

How your team handles *Set* will determine whether culture change is activated or blocked.

Identify the Levers of Change

Trajectories towards more constructive outcomes require a swerve in practice. A swerve is an alteration from the way things are currently going.

Ritualize readiness – we need to signal and commit to one another that we are ready to shift gears.

In work teams, a 'one word' round. Each team member says a word that represents how they want to show up today.

People perform better when they feel they're contributing to something bigger than themselves. In high-performing teams – on the sports ground or in the office – there's often a shared narrative, a culture that sounds like:

- *We back each other.*
- *We provide impeccable service.*
- *We own our role, and trust others to do the same.*
- *We are creating the best school possible.*

Shift Minds Through Action

The quickest way to calm the mind is to exert the body. Physiology affects psychology.

Pre-game routines reduce cortisol and increase testosterone, boosting confidence. For example, boxers using strong, confident body language before stepping into the ring feel more dominant. While is not something often sued in schools, it should be. When people act together, they tend to think together.

Physiological Resets

Use breathing to reset physiology (Box breathing, or '3–6–5': 3 seconds inhale, 6 hold, 5 exhale, humming, chanting).

Deploy 'go-to' recovery rituals: for example, clapping reset, quick team huddle, visualizing past success.

Train 'second point' thinking. This goes beyond initial reactions to thinking about the next best action. For example, a leader or coach might say, *Let's not lose the next moment worrying about the last issue.* or *We can't change that – we can shift this.*

Rapid Recovery Techniques

Use breathing and body cues. Coach team members to slow their breathing and increase their focus by attaining an alpha brain wave state, repeating affirmations or taking one grounding breath.

High-performing teams build a linked neurobiology, their nervous systems sync when we feel CPR. The best teams don't just plan together, they breathe, laugh and recalibrate together before they act.

Ways to sync:

- Grounding rituals (breathing, music, chants).
- Warm-ups that include playful or *bonding* elements.
- Humour.

Pressure Test a New Approach

While we have a strategy and a plan, we need to test it to see if it works. Conduct a pre-mortem. Predict what could go wrong. What setbacks might we face. Record everything that happens. Collect data. Create knowledge. Refine strategy. Refine your strategy and processes rather than focusing on results.

Setting up a brief 'burst' period to pressure test the plan and if it is not working re-adjust.

Reframe Threats as Challenges

Culture shifts often stall because fear, fatigue or frustration impair decision-making. Instead of focusing on the past, focus on what needs to be done to accomplish success.

This relates to Albert Bandura's research on collective efficacy where teams

- Set goals.
- Persist in the face of obstacles.
- Solve problems.
- Recover from setbacks.

Collective efficacy is not simply the sum of individual team members' self-efficacy beliefs. It emerges from shared perceptions and interaction patterns and can be higher or lower than the average of the team member's self-efficacies.

Setbacks Feed Ingenuity – They Don't Define Identity

Teams that reframe setbacks as learning moments rebound faster.

This is just the preliminary stage. Let's gather intelligence about what works to we can exert this more powerfully in the future.

Fear of losing decreases when setbacks are viewed as feedback, not personal inadequacy.

We can only control the things that are under our control. If we get the processes right, we will experience compounding gains.

Twerk and Lurk

What is a small thing that we could do that would:

Change our view of ourselves; and
Cause anyone watching us to pause for thought and consider that the balance has shifted.

Try it and gain information from its effects.

If *set* is skipped, what follows is often chaotic coordination, blame-shifting or hesitancy, momentum's greatest enemies.

Withstanding the First Setback

Reframe setbacks fast. Avoid blame; offer immediate perspective: *That didn't land. Reset. What's next?* We need to protect one another when this occurs.

Mike Tyson's famous quote is that everyone has a plan until they are punched on their nose. We need to plan out what to do after the first biff on our nose.

Any ambitious undertaking involves setbacks. Anything really worth doing involves taking chances and overcoming challenges.

Setbacks are not opposite of success but a necessary stepping stone towards it. What matters is how we respond to them. If we misinterpret setbacks as failures, we can consolidate a sense of inability and stifle success.

Rather than viewing setbacks as something to be feared or avoided, embrace them as a natural part of the process of improving school culture.

Resilience is the ability to bungy-jump back from challenges and adversity, and it is a crucial trait for achieving long-term success. The most successful people are often those who have experienced the most failure but have continued to persist.

We all face times of adversity. A single setback should not define your overall journey or deter you from pursuing your goals.

Successful people understand that failure is temporary and part of the process.

Set is an incredible opportunity. It is the 'pre-performance window'. If a team tends to blame one another under pressure, cortisol (stress hormone) surges, energy slumps and attention narrows.

This is why the culture of any team is critical. The way we do anything is the way we do everything. With the right tools, teams can reset emotionally, realign mentally and enter a flow state together.

Teams that master *Ready, Set, Go* don't just win – they build cultures of resilience, fire and flow.

Set is often rushed or skipped in busy teams. But it's sacred. It's the moment where fear either fractures the team or forges them. By naming fears, syncing emotional states, and anchoring to a courageous identity, leaders help their teams transform hesitation into momentum.

The best teams don't just survive the tension of *Set* – they use it as a springboard.

Noticing pivotal moments and capitalizing on them is important in all of our lives.

Changing the Odds

> *There is a tide in the affairs of men (and women)*
>
> *Which, taken at the flood, leads on to fortune;*
>
> *Omitted, all the voyage of their life*
>
> *Is bound in shallows and in miseries.*
>
> *On such a full sea are we now afloat;*
>
> *And we must take the current when it serves,*
>
> *Or lose our ventures.* (William Shakespeare, *Julius Caesar*)

During World War that tide shifted. On Crete, Nazi soldiers encountered the Australian and New Zealand forces. The Aussie's started coo-eeing one another, a sound unfamiliar to the Nazis. Then the New Zealand troops started a haka. The Nazi soldiers fled. For the local people this was the first indication that the invading Nazis could be scared and beaten. Collectively they created a shift in beliefs and efficacy.

Go is when trust converts into action. It's where energy translates into execution. And it's where the best teams show their true strength – not because they never lose momentum, but because they know how to recover it.

This is where everything the team has built in *Ready* and *Set* is put into motion to scale up success. But as every coach and team leader knows, the launch is only half the battle.

Success Spirals

Cultural improvements build with respect, rhythm, confidence and connection – but can collapse in an instant.

Positive momentum spreads through our collective mirror neurons and amplifies through energy contagion. When we see someone express enthusiasm or confidence, our mirror neurons fire in a way that causes us to feel it too. Feelings are contagious.

During the *Go* phase, a fired-up team member can literally shift the physiology of others. When a team becomes unified in achieving outcomes, it is connected not just at a mindset level; it has a shared physiology and nervous system.

Leverage points result in the fastest gains at a ratio of 85:15. This is where the fastest learning occurs: 85% of the time we stick to our known brand and play to our strengths; 15% of the time we do the creative and the unexpected.

Micro-Shifts

We take our synchrony between team members and then consolidate with shared intentionality. Micro-shifts are small, measurable alterations we make to the way we achieve outcomes. Micro-accomplishments build belief and reinforce a sense of capacity.

Start Fast, But Don't Rush

Successful cultural change loves clarity and action. Great teams begin with quick wins – a solid play, a solved problem, a confident exchange.

Early success increases confidence, which then boosts dopamine.

But this doesn't mean frantic activity. It means decisive, intentional movement. In sports, execute the first play cleanly. In schools hit that first milestone. Win the moment, to build belief.

Surge Points

Now is the moment to upscale and surge ahead. Amplify intensity of purposeful action in short bursts.

Capitalize on progress, ignite belief and sustain flow and energy. Move fast. Trust your instincts. During surge times, let the leaders within your team lead. They will drive communication in the moment.

A school leader's role is to recognize and reinforce momentum signs. Provide support from the sideline, staying calm but activated. Use posture, tone and eye contact to send belief.

Always act in a manner that models how you want your team to treat people.

Power Up

Teams with positive emotional contagion perform better under stress, recover from setbacks faster and report higher satisfaction.

Leaders who display high-energy positivity influence the mood tone of the whole group.

In workplaces and sport, energy leaders are often the turning point in momentum shifts.

Positivity doesn't just turn the tide; it makes people smarter, faster and more aligned.

Positive contagion of energy occurs when emotions, attitudes and behaviours ripple through a team. Positive emotions broaden attention and thinking, improving creativity, decision-making and coordination.

When energy is contagious, teams act faster, trust more and sustain higher effort over time.

- High-performing teams share specific non-verbal energy micro-signals.

- High face-to-face interaction.
- Rapid turn-taking in speech.
- High levels of physical energy and movement.

These micro-signals predict performance better than content or IQ. How we talk to one another matters more than what we say.

There are four main indicators, leaders and coaches can use to gauge whether positive contagion is working:

1. *Interaction synchrony*: How connected and in-sync people are in conversations (tone, rhythm, responsiveness). High-performing teams have rapid turn-taking and rhythm. They tend to mirror each other's posture, tone and pace. Decisions feel smooth, indicating engagement and trust. Differences are deliberated on and resolved.
2. *Activity level/energy*: The physical and vocal energy people bring to interactions revs up. There is an increase of energy (frequent speaking, animated gestures, upright posture). Energetic individuals set the emotional tone of the group. People feel safe with one another.
3. *Fluidity of influence*: In high-performing teams, it is sometimes difficult to know exactly who the leader is. Everyone is expected to contribute and their contribution is respected.

Engagement flows in all directions – not just from the people in formalized leadership roles. Teams with distributed influence (not bottlenecked in one leader) keep flexible under pressure.

People who get others to respond, shift position or speak more have higher influence.

4. *Post-performance*: Conducting a review of the high-energy moments and the pivotal points in an undertaking empowers us to replicate success patterns.

READY. SET. GO. THE MAP

Effective enduring cultural change is the belief that 'things are going our way' leads to greater effort and focus. Success breeds confidence, which increases motivation (success-motivation loop).

This starts with tiny wins and catalytic actions. Small, visible progress in meaningful tasks leads to the highest boosts in engagement, creativity, and performance. Micro-accomplishments build belief and reinforce a sense of capability. Momentum builds faster when effort feels noticed and meaningful (see Fig. 7).

In the *Go* phase, teams need to:

- Feel traction.
- See success accumulating.
- Maintain emotional lift.
- Reduce friction.

Mood drives effort. Effort drives results. Results drive mood. This builds team efficacy.

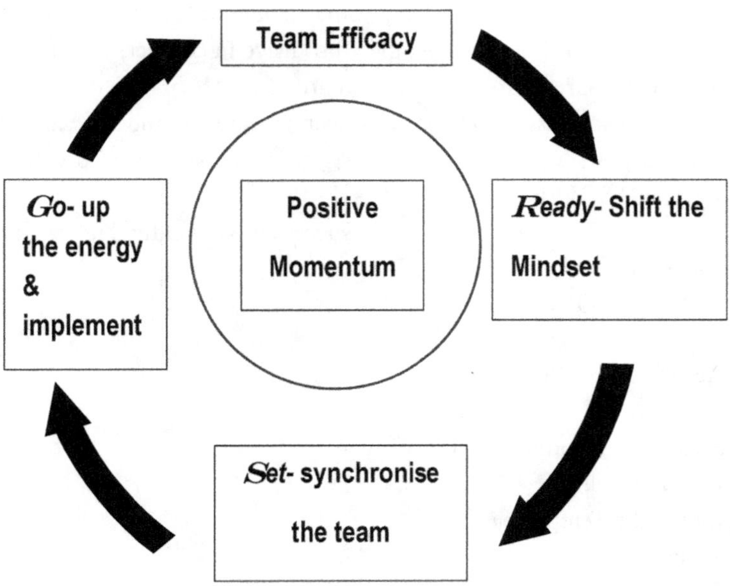

Fig. 7 Ready. Set. Go.

TRICKY CONVERSATIONS

When you set about changing a school culture, not everyone is going to be thrilled. Some people will be pessimistic about your chances of success (generally these are the 'possessors of privilege' – they have benefitted from the way things have been previously). Some will remain silent, anticipating that you will join a long list of leaders who had good intentions but failed miserably.

Other will be more flagrantly antagonistic to your new-fangled ways. The immune barrier in schools sometimes sounds like, 'We tried that in 2020. It didn't work then and it's not going to work now'.

Tricky conversations aren't just something you need to expect and prepare for, they are often a sign that you a creating an impact.

Mark Twain once said, *The only people who like changes are babies* (and we're not even sure babies are that fond of them).

Given that you are undertaking change, you can expect to ruffle some feathers, put some noses put out of joint and to bruise some egos. As a result, you will have some tricky conversations. Unless you are one of those rare people who thrive in conflict, you might need to prepare yourself for this eventually.

Let's discuss a model that has been researched and refined for over 35 years and provides the basis of our most requested workshop – RESOLVE.

RESOLVE is a model for successfully conducting tricky conversations.

The RESOLVE model is:

Respond with Respect
Engage
Seek understanding
Observe feelings
Lower the Temperature
Value add
Empower.

Respond with Respect

Aim to respond rather than react. If we react, we are being led by an upset person's actions. Responding involves leading and calming angry people. Try to give people what they need, not what they deserve.

Anger is a form of poison. If you absorb it, it will have to be removed later on. If you become angry yourself, consider, 'Who will be infected by this anger – my family? My friends?'

The key in calming angry people lies in respect. Feeling respected creates the sense of being heard and increases trust. Feelings of trust reduce anger. When we respond respectfully, we enable angry people to calm and recover.

We convey respect by deeply listening. Even when our strong inclination is to dispute an accusation, become quiet.

Engage

A guiding rule in any relationship is, if one of us has a problem, we have a problem. Create a safe location. Ask people to sit down with you and explain what is happening for them.

The only comments you will make will be to ask clarifying questions. Your only job is to find out where they are hurting.

People often start with a complaint that is not reflective of their true feelings. Many people rehearse a confrontation in their minds many times before talking it through. They don't only rehearse their issue, but they also imagine your replies and then their replies to your imagined replies. The simplest way to not fall into this is to only ask questions.

Have a code of conduct when you are helping upset people. Be humble. Be kind. Consider that behind all of this upset and complaint, is a person who is hurting. If one person refuses to struggle or engage in the conflict, there can be no conflict.

Instead, you might say,

I am really sorry this has happened.

I am glad you let me know.

(Sometimes you may ask, *Is this something you want me to help you work out or do you just want me to know about it?*)

Let's see what we can do to solve it.

Eighty per cent of communication is non-verbal. What you do is more important than what you say.

While sitting down is ideal, if you are standing, be at an angle (45 degrees) with your right-side forwards rather than directly fronting the person can help keep a situation calm and non-adversarial.

Hold your hands in front of you in a temple position to communicate calm authority.

People's feet often give more information than their faces. Usually, feet point in the direction the person is most likely to move next. A shift in the direction may give you an early warning that someone is about to run away, leave or move closer to you.

Maintain at least one and a half arm's length distance from the upset person. This is less likely to increase the person's anxiety. You will also reduce danger to yourself by giving yourself time to react to sudden moves.

Position yourself so you are safe. If you can, place something between you. Find safer ground. If they back away, slowly retreat also. If they start to come back, stop and wait.

Seek Understanding

Listening and validating concerns, communicates respect. Validating doesn't necessarily mean agreeing; it means acknowledging the distress or upset behind the immediate issue.

Try to listen in three ways:

1. Listen for content (what's being said).
2. Listen for process (how they are saying it and why).
3. Listen for intervention (what to do about it).

If someone approaches you looking irate, be the first one to talk. Say, 'Hi, you look upset about something. Can we talk about it?'

Acknowledging their feelings at the outset prevents the person from feeling the need to prove how they feel, by demonstrating it. Where possible, invite them to move with you away from main thoroughfares.

Talking and calming are incompatible. If you try to verbally explain or defend yourself while trying to calm the other person, you will send mixed messages. It is never wise to send mixed messages to angry people.

It is impossible to simultaneously calm someone down, get them back onside and convince them that the whole thing is not really your fault all at the same time.

Try to re-direct their verbal aggression into a problem-solving approach.

Observe Feelings

By the time an upset person gets to you, they're already frustrated. They may not be interested in solutions. They may just want someone they can yell at to vent their anger.

Upset people are often in rush to express & share their displeasure. Slow down the process. Give them the sense that you have plenty of time to hear them out.

Lower levels of stress but do not make a joke. People who are angry cannot be joked out of it. People may increase their anger if they feel they are not being taken seriously. People often stop yelling when you calmly and quietly ask, 'Could you please speak a little slower, I'd like to understand?'

Repeating back to the other person what was said also does this. Listen then paraphrase.

To cool things down, do something unexpected. Ask the person to sit down or step away yourself to get something, like a pen to take notes. Offer them a glass of water or a cup of tea. If all else fails, excuse yourself & act as if you're about to sneeze.

Lower the Temperature

In some ways, calming an angry person is similar to protecting yourself from an aggressive animal:

Aim to give the message that you aren't really a threat.
Avoid direct eye contact – glance but don't stare.
Speak only in a calm voice.

'Be a tree' with feet together, elbows against your chest and keep hands still, by your sides or on your chest. Lower the level of tension, stimulation and adrenaline. Breathe evenly.

Lowering the tone also involves being aware of the neurochemistry of upset.

Two neurochemicals that are often present in upsets:

Cortisol and Adrenaline.

These can cause people to have a steely focus without necessarily being able to think their way towards a solution. Reducing these will help you to shift towards calmness. Some ways include:

- Increasing certainty (what I'd like to do next is ...).
- Drinking water.
- Walking beside someone (if safe to do so) Asking people to map out an action plan including the key steps.
- Calm and attentive listening.
- Reassurance that they are being taken seriously and that this issue can be sorted out.

Two neurochemicals that are often lessened during upsets:
Dopamine and Serotonin
We can increase these by:

- Giving positive feedback, for example, 'I understand we have an issue to solve but I want to thank you for being direct enough to bring it to me so we can start to find a solution'. Emphasizing points of agreement.
- Giving choices, for example, specify the key issues as you see them. Check it with them. Then ask them which one they would like to discuss first.

Value Add

Ask, 'What would you like me to do?' or 'How can I help you?'

This unexpected question is the most useful tool for dealing with anger. Upset people.

During an outburst, useful information can be gained. Listen for the feelings behind the facts. Restate the message you think you have received in order to determine if you correctly understood the person. Either don't know or won't admit what they want you to do. To answer this question, they will have to stop and think, which is what you want them to do.

When it is appropriate (and it isn't always) allow the person to release as much energy as possible by venting verbally. As a person is venting, there will be peaks and valleys in the outburst. If you cannot allow the person to continue venting, state the limits during the 'valleys' in the venting process.

Empower

Your gut feeling of fear is something you should attend to. No animal senses fear and thinks *oh, it is nothing*. If you are in a loop and getting nowhere ask someone else to take over. If you really feel unsafe with someone leave.

FOR REFLECTION AND DISCUSSION

1. Who did you learn most of your conflict resolution models from?
2. How successful was that model?
3. Is it the best model you could use?
4. Who is the best coach you've ever heard of or witnessed?
5. Did they management to turn a team around or create a momentum shift?
6. How did they do this?
7. Can you apply this to your own life?

KEY IDEAS

- In creating a CPR culture, leaders are often in the role of coaches.
- Successful coaches often leverage the positive forces within the teams they coach.
- We use the model of the familiar – Ready, set, go to typify this process.
- Positive changes almost invariably create a backlash. There is a human inclination to return to homeostasis (the way things have always been).
- For this reason, the more you embark on cultural change the most likely it is that you will be invited by others to engage in tricky conversations.
- As most of us dislike conflict, we are often ill-prepared for these conversations.
- RESOLVE is a methodology you can use to conduct these conversations.

10

THE CONNECTED, PROTECTED AND RESPECTED (CPR) APPROACH TO SCHOOL CULTURE: FINAL REFLECTIONS

This book has been written at a time when the world feels poised on a precipice. The tectonic plates of the times are shifting, and we face strong cross currents. The challenge for school leaders is how to navigate through these times successfully.

Before discussing how to curate and steer schools through these times, we'll examine some of the conflicting forces impacting on schools. Between them the authors have collectively assisted thousands of schools and education systems throughout the world. Such experiences have strongly informed the perspectives presented in our book.

School leaders have a multiplicity of roles – drivers of improvement, educators, energizers, enablers and supporters (Edwards et al., 2022). Already the complexity of their roles risks depleting the capacity of even the most energetic of leaders.

One aim of connected, protected and respected (CPR) is to create and maintain sustainable cultures rather than risk losing our most capable leaders and educators. Without it, the level of collateral damage is alarming.

Not only are good people wishing to leave the profession, but talented educators sometimes feel reluctant to step up into leadership positions.

THE WARNING BELLS

Depending on where you are located, there are existing and concerning trends in terms of lowered staff morale, increased absenteeism and sick leave, and heightened mental health fragility. We could propose that we need to better prepare our educators for the challenges they will face and leaders for the complexities they need to resolve. As useful as those attempts can be, they will never be enough.

This is not an issue of personal deficiency in either your capacity as a leader or in the staff you lead. This is not just a lack of personal capacity or skill or 'grit' or resilience of the people working in schools. It is a design issue.

What we see are leaders and educators working harder than ever in a system that is no longer designed in a way that is 'fit for purpose'.

Let's review just a few of the indicators.

AI AND AGI

The accelerating and exponential impacts of AI and generative AI provide a catalyst to the ways people can learn and problem solve. Contained within it are promises, possibilities and perils. Adapting successfully to these challenges while maximizing the opportunities, confronts all school leaders. We need to prepare our students for futures that will not be easily replaced by AGI. They will need a different range of mindsets, skillsets and toolsets to capitalize on opportunities in their future.

DYSREGULATION

We live in tumultuous times. People are more easily dysregulated. Large-scale studies of student wellbeing (Skodel, 2026) indicate increasing levels of anxiety, feelings of loneliness, feelings of being overloaded and mood disorder. There is a greater emphasis on online, and app-based mental health supports, but this has not lessened the demand for school mental health support services. Wellbeing programmes in schools have limited, if any, impact (ACER, 2020).

These studies also indicate that educators are experiencing higher levels of burnout, exhaustion, anxiety and lower levels of psychological safety in their workplaces.

The cumulative effect of increased distress and disturbance among students and staff results in school leaders spending more time containing dysregulation than designing learning.

There is a greater diversity of students in terms of readiness, levels of academic competence and engagement. In addition, an increased proportion of the student population are being diagnosed as neurodiverse. Official figures suggest this is around 20% of the school population, but our own impression is that the real rate is higher.

Educators aim to provide accommodations and modifications to meet the learning needs of these students. While their efforts are commendable, it is becoming increasingly obvious that a single delivery or instructional model fits fewer students well.

Essentially, this means that school leaders and their educators are being asked to provide personalized learning within structures designed for standardization. This results in an almost breathless, relentless pressure for educators to cover and 'get though' the curriculum rather than having time to impart the latest research and knowledge. While educational academics intensely debate the relative merits of different instructional methodologies, this risks missing the main point, schools can only stretch their existing systems and structures, so far. It is time for a re-design.

To conclude our review of indicators, let's raise something is difficult to research accurately but is easy to see. The aftermath of the COVID years includes a greater emphasis on individualism and a wariness about collaboration.

TEAMWORK

Almost any enduring positive gains that occur in schools are a product of teams who work together and build a culture that supports constructive improvements. Effective teamwork is based on quality relationships. As outlined in Chapter 2, it involves building trust, forgiveness, hope, integrity and kindness.

These are human relational qualities. They cannot be outsourced to a website or downloaded in the form of an app. Effective teams make work easier by sharing the load and supporting one another. It involves communication, planning, decision-making, resolving tricky conversations, strength-building and collaboration. At its core, it is these relationships that make a school's culture.

Generally, people have returned from the COVID years, less well equipped to know how to be constructive team members. Despite being in a world that is shifting from individual ability to collective intelligence, encouraging and modelling how to be a constructive team member requires leadership.

THE CPR OF SCHOOL CULTURE

The acronym of CPR to summarize the key ingredients of a positive school culture is one that people find memorable. Creating sustainable messaging around this theme is straightforward.

In the many workshops we have conducted with leaders on this topic, not one person has questioned this framework. Based on extensive research, it also has immediate face validity and provides an actionable framework for leaders to begin the process of redesigning their schools. The reason is that it feels 'real' – it resonates with the experiences of people.

CPR also aligns with core psychological needs. We all need some form of connectedness in our lives, we all need to feel safe and secure, and we all hope to be respected for who we are and the meaningful activities we undertake. We need our hopes and dreams to be nurtured rather than crushed.

Adaptive leadership is nuanced, human and flexible. It favours the relational aspects of leadership without neglecting the technical requirements.

Throughout this book, we have emphasized the need to know your school – to complete a thorough diagnosis of the situation before intervening. As Stephen is fond of saying, *If you can't read the room, you can't lead the room.*

Whether your assessment is that your school culture could be in ICU with a barely detectable heartbeat, and in need of urgent resuscitation, or whether it is simply needing a day spa to spruce up a few aspects of functioning, CPR remains relevant.

At the risk of being repetitive, however, be careful of over-personalizing the challenges you face rather than facing up to the need to re-design. CPR can be a framework you use to re-design:

- Utilization of AI and AGI.
- Importing the latest brain research on learning to create meaningful and effective cognitive architecture in your school.
- Regulation is an essential precursor to learning and effective action.
- Teamwork

WHY CPR WORKS WELL AS A SCHOOL MODEL

Based on research with 193,000 students, CPR creates a shared language for leaders, teachers, parents and students. It is inclusive of all types of learners and recognizes that wellbeing and optimal learning and performance are inseparable. They are the twin strands of the DNA of great schools.

The CPR framework is broad enough to encompass a range of approaches including trauma-informed, attachment-aware and how to build expertise and self-efficacy in school communities. Regardless of whether schools prefer a didactic approach to teaching or a more student-centred one, CPR applies.

CPR is not a programme. It is framework that assists you in re-designing schools.

While compatible with most existing approaches, CPR emphasizes a few key elements.

School cultures are living systems that should never be reduced to mechanistic processes where people are replaceable cogs in a system that values outcomes over quality processes. This takes CPR from an interesting model to a practical, actionable process for intervention.

This expands leadership from technical guide or stewardship or even lead learner to a role where the aim is to animate, re-invigorate and enthuse their community. CPR provides a tonic to school communities. It is the antidote to a system that works more for accountability and standardization over relationships, regulation and recovery.

Given some of the deflated, lethargic, and risk-adverse school cultures we have worked alongside leaders to transform, it is shocking to contemplate the capital that had been squandered or suppressed in some schools. The collective energy of all those young people, the hopes and dreams of their parents and the eagerness of educators at times was reduced to a sense of sullen complaint drudgery.

We should all be appalled by such an outcome and then to use it as a salutary lesson to reawaken the enthusiasm in our community. In this sense, leaders are chief enthusiasts.

Education should not be an exercise in exhaustion. It should enliven people and enlarge possibilities.

Central concepts to enlivening and redesigning our school culture are:

Connected:

- Relationships are central to quality school cultures. To aim towards high rigour, we need to recognize that relationships always come first.
- Relationships are related to regulation. Most of us do not self-regulate when we are calm or distressed, we co-regulate.
- A culture that helps people to regulate and recover promotes learning.
- Belonging and connecting is a powerful way of building mental health and wellbeing.
- Feedback, collaboration, sharing or ideas, coaching, restorative conversations are essential elements.
- Like great teams, great schools are ones where everyone contributes.

- Collective intelligence and problem-solving are valued.

Protected:

- People cannot learn optimally when they are dysregulated, stressed or fearful.
- Parents are well-intended but often fearful. By helping them to realize the journey of childhood development and the journey of education, they can be less stressed by the accomplishments and challenges inherent in any learning journey. When parents feel less anxious, their children feel more secure and adventurous. They are willing to 'have-a-go'. When students feel less anxious, they are less likely to behave in ways that seem self-protective but ultimately are self-damaging. When students enjoy learning more, educators become more relaxed. When educators feel calmer and more confident and creative, school leaders can also be less frantic and frenzied.
- Predictability and routines are kindness.
- Outlining a developmental journey builds a sense of calm progression for all students.
- Trauma-informed practice, adult emotional regulation.

Respected:

- Everyone contributes.
- Everyone has different learning strengths. There isn't one way of being smart. People learn and develop skills in different areas and in different ways.
- Strength-based teaching, design thinking, data literacy and learning strengths are used to differentiate. A motto we would like to suggest is *Here Everyone Gets Smart* (and they will get smart in different ways because they have different brains).
- Choice boards, co-designed rubrics, innovation sprints.

We reinterpret these dimensions through the core human needs that shape learning cultures:

- CONNECTED → builds relationships, belonging, collaboration.
- PROTECTED → increases the sense of safety, predictability, clarity, wellbeing.
- RESPECTED → empowers empowerment, voice, challenge, growth.

CONNECTED CULTURE

Psychological anchor: Belonging, community, relational trust.

What this looks like in a school:

- High-relational trust between teachers, leaders, students and families.
- Collaboration over competition.
- Shared rituals, team identity, peer support structures.
- Strong induction systems for new staff and new students.
- Mentoring and co-teaching encouraged.
- High levels of psychological safety.

Strengths:

- High engagement, lower burnout, supportive climate, improved wellbeing.

Risks if overplayed:

- Avoidance of difficult conversations.
- Slow decision-making.
- 'Niceness' over accountability.

THE PROTECTED CULTURE

Psychological anchor: Safety, clarity, boundaries, consistency.

What this looks like in a school:

- Clear policies and consistent behaviour expectations.
- Well-established routines and predictable learning environments.
- Strong safeguarding practices.
- Data are reliable, processes repeatable.
- Timetables, procedures and communication are orderly.
- Teachers feel that chaos is contained.
- Students know 'what happens next'.

Strengths:

- Predictability reduces anxiety, especially for neurodivergent students.
- Efficient operations increase time for teaching and learning.

Risks if overplayed:

- Bureaucracy, rigidity, rule-following over responsiveness.
- Staff feel micromanaged.
- Creativity and initiative decline.

THE RESPECTED CULTURE

Psychological anchor: Identity and character formation, agency, being valued for not just what you bring bit who you are and who you can become.

What this looks like in a school:

- Teachers trusted with autonomy in instructional design.
- Students empowered with choice, voice and agency.
- Innovation and experimentation encouraged.
- High expectations with celebration of growth and excellence.
- Professional learning cultures where expertise is admired, not feared.
- Data used for improvement, not punishment.

Strengths:

- High performance, creativity and innovation.
- Students and teachers feel empowered and capable.

Risks if overplayed:

- Overemphasis on achievement → pressure and competition.
- Innovation without support → burnout.
- Risk of fragmentation.

Leading a CPR culture requires the development of emotional intelligence beginning with the leadership team and then creating a resonant way of relating that ripples through the school. Ideally this simply becomes the way we do things here- this is the way we treat one another.

To assist you in preparing yourself for introducing CPR, we ask you to reflect upon the following 20 questions:

1. Am I leading by example in everything I do? Reflects on whether actions consistently align with values and expectations set for the team.
2. How effectively am I communicating my vision and goals to my team? Ensure that the mission and objectives are clear, inspiring, and understood by everyone.

3. Am I actively listening to my team and valuing their input? Self-checks on whether input is genuinely sought and considered in decision-making.
4. Am I challenging myself and my team to innovate and improve? Encourages a focus on growth, innovation and continuous improvement.
5. What's one skill or area I need to improve to be a more effective leader? Promote self-awareness and a commitment to personal development.
6. Am I fostering a culture of trust and accountability within my team? Examine the environment for openness, reliability, and responsibility.
7. Do I understand the individual learning strengths, goals, and challenges of each team member? Reflects on relationship-building and personalized support.
8. Am I delegating effectively, or am I micromanaging? Ensures a balance between oversight and empowering the team.
9. How am I supporting diversity, equity, and inclusion in my leadership practices? Ensure commitment to a diverse and supportive workplace.
10. Am I making decisions based on data, intuition or both? Encourages balanced, informed decision-making.
11. What values am I prioritizing in my decision-making process? Help clarify whether decisions align with core organizational values.
12. How well am I managing my time and energy? Addresses personal efficiency and prioritization for sustainable leadership.
13. Do I provide timely, constructive feedback and am I open to receiving feedback myself? Emphasize feedback culture and openness to personal growth.
14. Am I celebrating successes, both big and small, with my team? Ensure that recognition and appreciation are part of the workplace.
15. What legacy am I building as a leader? Encourage a long-term perspective on the impact and influence of leadership.
16. How well am I adapting to change and helping my team do the same? Assesses resilience and adaptability in a dynamic environment.

17. Am I aware of, reflecting on and managing my own biases? Promotes self-awareness and fairness in interactions and decisions.
18. How transparent am I with my team about decisions and changes? Reflects on the importance of openness and trust-building through transparency.
19. Am I nurturing future leaders within my team? Ensures focus on mentoring, coaching and developing others for leadership.
20. Am I developing myself and my people for a rapidly changing future or am I at risk of preparing them for a world that no longer exists?

OUR VISION

We hope to work with as many schools as we possibly can to create CPR – the conditions in which people thrive. At the heart of this process are the school leaders who will be the catalyst for change.

CPR incorporates the optimal conditions for neuroplasticity and positive identity/character development.

We aim to have all people in education develop the confidence and the skills they will need to create and contribute to a better world.

To do this they need to feel supported to develop the mind-sets, skillsets and toolsets that equip them to flourish in a changed world.

The skills that the World Economic Forum (2025) estimates will be most in demand in the future are:

- Creative thinking.
- Analytical thinking.
- Technological literacy.
- Curiosity and lifelong learning.
- Resilience, flexibility and agility.
- Systems thinking.
- AI and big data.

- Motivation and self-efficacy.
- Talent management (and team building).
- Customer/client service

We think CPR provides a practical framework for achieving these capacities. We invite you to dream with us and work with us.

REFERENCES

ACER. (2020).*A systematic review of intervention research examining effective student wellbeing in schools and their academic outcomes.* https://research.acer.edu.au/well_being/14/

Edwards, E., Cave, W., Bissell, S., & Barrie, J. (2022, December). *Supporting primary school principals to manage complexity in contemporary education settings applying a service lens to support education leadership for the Australian Government Primary Principal Association (AGPPA).* https://agppa.asn.au/wp-content/uploads/2023/03/Applying-a-Service-Lens-to-Support-Primary-Education-Leadership_Research-Report-Summary_Dec22.pdf

Skodel. (2026). *Personal communication and internal analysis.* https://skodel.com/

World Economic Forum. (2025). *Future of jobs report 2025: The jobs of the future – and the skills you need to get them.* https://www.weforum.org/stories/2025/01/future-of-jobs-report-2025-jobs-of-the-future-and-the-skills-you-need-to-get-them/

ABOUT THE AUTHORS

Stephen Brown is an internationally renowned thought leader, scholar practitioner, a highly respected education system executive and consultant. He is at the cutting edge of research, practice and development of school leaders. He has an outstanding reputation for leading and supporting sustainable cultural change from whole system to individual schools.

Andrew Fuller focuses on helping schools create futures for people they can fall in love with. His work on Neuro Advantage and learning strengths draws together the latest approaches in systems thinking, learning design and cognitive architecture. He is a clinical psychologist and author who has helped guide school leaders in the UK, Asia, Africa, New Zealand and Australia.

www.ingramcontent.com/pod-product-compliance
Lightning Source LLC
LaVergne TN
LVHW012336130926
847902LV00028B/412
* 9 7 8 1 8 3 7 4 2 0 9 6 4 *